Book Of Mormon Contradictions

Joseph's Book is Put On Trial With The Bible

Paul Gee

Contents

Introduction

The Book of Mormon is placed in the courtroom of scrutiny, with the Bible as the source of truth. Each individual verse in the Book of Mormon is effectively put on trial. The Bible serves as the frame of reference for the trial at hand. This is very important, as we do not want to be led astray through a fictional book that is said to be scripture. In saying this, I have compared the verses in the Book of Mormon with the Bible and found that many verses disagree with the Biblical text. These verses will be looked over in great detail, in order to properly understand the issues we are dealing with. Instead of the two books complimenting each other, we see them contradicting one another in many ways. An in-depth analysis of the Book of Mormon shows a substantial amount of problems that cannot be denied. As you traverse through the chapters of this book, the problems in the Book of Mormon will be readily seen. These disparities come to life, seeing what the Bible actually teaches compared to the Book of Mormon. Most teachings are not the same. If they are, then they contradict the teachings in Mormonism.

As we read each chapter in this book, it will become increasingly apparent that there are theological issues in the Book of Mormon. In fact, we see that it contradicts the Bible and hardly ever compliments it. There are even teachings found in the Book of Mormon that Christians would believe in, but LDS people would not. These verses are also mentioned in detail when compared to the core doctrines in Mormonism. Despite the Book of Mormon being hailed as Another Testament of Jesus Christ, it is seen as the opposite. False teachings and practices are seen at every glance. This causes a person to form false beliefs based on what the book says. This book's claim of being a sacred scripture, or God's Word comes under serious question. Therefore, a word of caution would be advisable against placing blind faith in the Book of Mormon. This is especially true since it lacks any evidence to its claims of an ancient book about an American people who lived here from 600BC to 400AD. These claims lack credibility without the discovery of manuscripts, cities, or people. Isn't it convenient that an angel supposedly took the Golden plates with him to heaven? What we have left is a book with Joseph Smith's beliefs, the same as what we see in the Joseph Smith Translation. Of course, Bible verses were added, along with parts about Jesus, to make it sound more Biblical.

I've seen too many people put their trust in the Book of Mormon just because they were brought up to believe in it. So let me be the first to say that our church's upbringing could be wrong. For this reason, it is important to look to Jesus and allow Him to be the Lord of our lives, and not man. Then, will people appreciate what God says in the Bible. His teachings will become a part of who we are and live by. As we put our trust in God, the Bible will become our firm foundation. This is where our belief system comes from. So when looking at the Book of Mormon, it should not trust it, as the text contradicts the Bible in many ways. If you are LDS, please know that Joseph's book is not of God. As for those who are looking into Mormonism, don't go down the path of reading the Book of Mormon. You will regret doing this in the long run. I will quote enough of this book for you to get the feel of it. There is enough evidence to demonstrate that the Book of Mormon is not of God. Nobody should trust it. Amen.

This book extends to two different websites. Check them out when you get a chance...

christvm.com **(Christianity Vs Mormonism):** Only Jesus Saves, Not Religion! There are hundreds of Mormon resources that are Free. It includes the Book of Mormon Contradictions, Plagiarism, Forbidden verses, and many other charts are available. Joseph Smith false prophecies, his wives, false beliefs in Mormonism and other resources are available. Books on the Book of Mormon This content has been available since 2016.

dailycdev.com **(Daily Christian Devotionals):** Growing Closer To Jesus Daily! There are thousands of Christian resources that are Free. It includes full length devotional messages, the Bible, Biblical truths, dozens of charts, videos, music, and more. For many years I wrote a new message from the Bible each day. Since then I have written three books that are available for Free on this site also. The content has been available since 2015.

Chapter 1

Baptism In The Church B.C.

In the Book of Mormon, we see a copycat of Acts, chapter 2. This chapter comes from Mosiah 18, and it is very much like the verses we see on the day of Pentecost in the Bible. See for yourself, as we read different verses. It is written, "yea, concerning that which was to come, and also concerning the resurrection of the dead, and the redemption of the people, which was to be brought to pass through the power, and sufferings, and death of Christ, and his resurrection and ascension into heaven." (Mosiah 18:2) "And he did teach them, and did preach unto them repentance, and redemption, and faith on the Lord." (Mosiah 18:7) "Now I say unto you, if this be the desire of your hearts, what have you against being baptized in the name of the Lord, as a witness before him that ye have entered into a covenant with him." (Mosiah 18:10) "And now when the people had heard these words, they clapped their hands for joy, and exclaimed: This is the desire of our hearts." (Mosiah 18:11) All this excitement over baptism supposedly occurred around a hundred and forty-five years before John the Baptist was born.

The story continues and says, "and after this manner he did baptize every one that went forth to the place of Mormon; and they were in number about two hundred and four souls." (Mosiah 18:16) So we see that over two hundred people got baptized on that day. How interesting that we don't see people doing sacrificial offerings at the tabernacle but had a church in their midst already. A very strange thing is seen in the verses as well. It talks about Jesus's suffering, along with His death and resurrection. How we are redeemed through Jesus's atonement for sins. Can anyone spot an issue here? Joseph Smith makes people believe that this knowledge of Jesus' sacrifice for sins was readily available before the birth of Jesus. Matthew speaks of Jesus coming into the world to take away our sins, but these specific details of Jesus being the last lamb to die for us was unknown till God came into this world. As for the church, it was not established in the Old Covenant timeframe. The talk of baptism happening in a church before John the Baptist is a big red flag, since the church began with Jesus.

The first recorded event of baptism by Immersion in the Bible is with John. This happened to be when Jesus started his ministry also. It is written, "and they asked him, and said unto him, Why baptizest thou then, if thou be not that Christ, nor Elias, neither that prophet? John answered them, saying, I baptize with water: but there standeth one among you, whom ye know not; He it is, who coming after me is preferred before me, whose shoe's latchet I am not worthy to unloose. These things were done in Bethabara beyond Jordan, where John was baptizing. The next day John seeth Jesus coming unto him, and saith, Behold the Lamb of God, which taketh away the sin of the world. This is he of whom I said, After me cometh a man which is preferred before me: for he was before me. And I knew him not: but that he should be made manifest to Israel, therefore am I come baptizing with water. And John bare record, saying, I saw the Spirit descending from heaven like a dove, and it abode upon him. And I knew him not: but he that sent me to baptize with water, the same said unto me, Upon whom thou shalt see the Spirit descending, and remaining on him, the same is he which baptizeth with the Holy Ghost." (John 1:25-33)

Baptism was also important in the church that Christ established. We see this on the day of Pentecost. Let's compare the events of the Book of Mormon with what the Bible says in Acts, chapter 2. It is written, "now when they heard this, they were pricked in their heart, and said unto Peter and to the rest of the apostles, Men and brethren, what shall we do? Then Peter said unto them, Repent, and be baptized every one of you in the name of Jesus Christ for the remission of sins, and ye shall receive the gift of the Holy Ghost. For the promise is unto you, and to your children, and to all that are afar off, even as many as the Lord our God shall call. And with many other words did he testify and exhort, saying, Save yourselves from this untoward generation. Then they that gladly received his word were baptized: and the same day there were added unto them about three thousand souls." (Acts 2:37-41) As we can see here, the story in Mosiah is very similar to what we see in Acts. It is like Joseph Smith took the story in Acts and rewrote it to match his story in the Book of Mormon. Unfortunately, this story in the Book of Mormon is not scripture. There is no evidence to back it up either.

As we read in Mosiah, the Book of Mormon and the Bible have conflicting information. Nobody was baptized in a church until Jesus set apart His church on earth. John the Baptist started baptizing for repentance, while baptism with the Holy Spirit started on the day of Pentecost in Acts 2. In ancient times, the Israelites followed the laws of Moses and did not have a church established. We also don't learn about baptism until John the Baptist came on the scene. Only ceremonial washings and water purifications are known. Isn't it interesting that Mosiah is supposedly recorded before Jesus's birth, in 147-145BC? This book demonstrates the need for baptism in Christ's church in the Old Testament times, where we don't see this in the Bible. Therefore, these people would have known better than to baptize for the remission of sins, as Jesus had not been born or sacrificed yet. At that timeframe, people could not see in the future and witness the death of Christ. The same knowledge about Jesus's resurrection and ascension into heaven was not written down as a vision either in the Old Testament portion of the Bible. Adding this information to the Book of Mormon suggests that people had special knowledge of things not present in the Bible. Here we see Joseph Smith attempting to make his book appear like it is prophesying of future events. However, it is only an attempt to make his book sound Biblical on paper. When comparing it with the Bible, we see how it is far from being of God. Amen.

Let us pray:

Oh Lord, I pray that LDS people will learn about the teachings of the Bible and not only depend on their church leaders for knowledge. I am grateful to be introduced to baptism through John the Baptist. Surely, this is when we see in scripture that people were repenting of their sins and turning to You, God. In the New Covenant, You brought about something amazing with baptism that was not present in the Old Covenant. Through baptism, we die to ourselves and rise with You as a new creation. You have made us alive in this darkened world.

People did not realize what they were missing out on until You came on the scene to save them. Thank You, Lord, for saving me. I pray that Your people will reach those who are lost There are millions of people in every country who are lost and in need of a Savior. Help deliver the Mormon people also from their false beliefs and to you for truth and knowledge. Then, can they come to You and be saved. Come Lord, Jesus. I love You. Amen.

Chapter 2

Baptism Is Necessary For Salvation

The Jesus of the Book of Mormon said that baptism is required to go to heaven. It is written, "verily, verily, I say unto you, that this is my doctrine, and I bear record of it from the Father; and whoso believeth in me believeth in the Father also; and unto him will the Father bear record of me, for he will visit him with fire and with the Holy Ghost. And thus will the Father bear record of me, and the Holy Ghost will bear record unto him of the Father and me; for the Father, and I, and the Holy Ghost are one. And again I say unto you, ye must repent, and become as a little child, and be baptized in my name, or ye can in nowise receive these things. And again I say unto you, ye must repent, and be baptized in my name, and become as a little child, or ye can in nowise inherit the kingdom of God." (3 Nephi 11:35-38) Here, we learn about the Holy Trinity, but baptism being required for salvation is unsound and extra Biblical.

What we just read goes against what Jesus of the Bible said. It is written, "go ye into all the world, and preach the gospel to every creature. He that believeth and is baptized shall be saved; but he that believeth not shall be damned. And these signs shall follow them that believe; In my name shall they cast out devils; they shall speak with new tongues; They shall take up serpents; and if they drink any deadly thing, it shall not hurt them; they shall lay hands on the sick, and they shall recover." (Mark 16:15-18) Does this mean that people who are not baptized are damned and don't go to heaven? Not at all. Jesus said that we are unsaved if we don't have faith in Him. Nowhere can we find in the Bible, where it says baptism is necessary for salvation. However, LDS people say it is and so does their sacred book, the Book of Mormon. But what is this book? It was manufactured by the hand of Joseph Smith and his friends. They made up this story, and added their own doctrines regarding baptism and other things in the text.

Joseph Smith fabricated fictional characters to declare his doctrines. How people must have faith, repent of their sins, be baptized, and receive the gift of the Holy Ghost to inherit the kingdom of God. Nowhere does the Bible say this. Baptism is important but not necessary for salvation. It is written, "for by grace are ye saved through faith; and that not of yourselves: it is the gift of God: Not of works, lest any man should boast." (Ephesians 2:8,9) Mormons would argue and say that baptism is required for salvation. They use these verses to back up that statement. It is written, "Jesus answered, Verily, verily, I say unto thee, Except a man be born of water and of the Spirit, he cannot enter into the kingdom of God. That which is born of the flesh is flesh; and that which is born of the Spirit is spirit." (John 3:5,6) What this really means is that we were born once in our mother's womb through water and blood. The second birth comes through the Holy Spirit. In Acts, chapter 2, it says that on the day of Pentecost, many people received the Holy Spirit through prayer, not through baptism.

"There was a man of the Pharisees, named Nicodemus, a ruler of the Jews: The same came to Jesus by night, and said unto him, Rabbi, we know that thou art a teacher come from God: for no man can do these miracles that thou doest, except God be with him. Jesus answered and said unto him, Verily, verily, I say unto thee, Except a man be born again, he cannot see the kingdom of God. Nicodemus saith unto him, How can a man be born when he is old? can he enter the second time into his mother's womb, and be born? Jesus answered, Verily, verily, I say unto thee, Except a man be born of water and of the Spirit, he cannot enter into the kingdom of God. That which is born of the flesh is flesh; and that which is born of the Spirit is spirit. Marvel not that I said unto thee, Ye must be born again. The wind bloweth where it listeth, and thou hearest the sound thereof, but canst not tell whence it cometh, and whither it goeth: so is every one that is born of the Spirit." (John 3:1-8)

Many people confuse John, chapter 3, and being born again of water with baptism of water. Therefore, they claim that a person must be baptized of water in order to be saved and go to heaven. However, this is not what the text says. Nicodemus mentioned to Jesus about the first birth. He knew that the first birth was coming out of our mother's womb, so he wanted to know what the second birth meant. Jesus said that in order to enter the kingdom of God, a person must be born again. This means being born of water (physical birth) and the Spirit. Our bodies have a spirit but to be led into all truth, we must receive the Holy Spirit. Think of the Spirit of God as our guide in this life. This is why Jesus said we must be born again in the Spirit to see and to enter the kingdom of God. When God's presence comes into our lives, Jesus is able to know us personally and spiritually. No longer are we led by the flesh, but by God also.

"And when he was demanded of the Pharisees, when the kingdom of God should come, he answered them and said, The kingdom of God cometh not with observation: Neither shall they say, Lo here! or, lo there! for, behold, the kingdom of God is within you." (Luke 17:20,21)

But where is the kingdom of God? Is it in heaven? How about paradise? Neither actually. Jesus said that people will look for the kingdom of God when in reality it is within us. God in us means that God is doing a work in us. We are different as God is leading us in life. This is kingdom work on earth as it is in heaven. It is also how a person is saved. If there is fruit from God's kingdom in our lives, then that means our faith is alive and active. For a surety, "by grace are ye saved through faith; and that not of yourselves: it is the gift of God: Not of works, lest any man should boast." (Ephesians 2:8,9) Our faith in Jesus us, not water baptism. This is why the thief on the cross went to paradise, having never been water baptized. But what if a person wants to be water baptized or has been, is that fine? Yes, of course. Water baptism refers to a person's willingness to commit their lives to follow Jesus. However, many people have done this without water baptism and are saved. Amen.

Let us pray:

Oh Lord, I pray that people will know how to distinguish between You, the real Jesus, and a fake one in other books. One thing I know is that You will never contradict Yourself, of which other writings outside the Bible often do. The Book of Mormon corrupts your Word.

The LDS people are hard-hearted and difficult to reach for Your kingdom. They have been trained from birth in what they believe to be true. So, as we come to share the gospel, many people don't accept it, even if it comes from the Bible. They prefer to believe what their modern-day prophets say rather than what the Bible says. Even more disturbing, they profess to be Christians. By so doing, they deceive many. How is it that they can wake up each day and feel like they are on Your side when they only believe in the Bible as far as it is translated correctly? They say the Book of Mormon is a perfect translation, even though there are no golden plates or evidence to support it. In so doing, they show blind faith, where they walk blindly on the path of destruction. I truly want to reach them with the truth, God. Therefore, lead me to people who are ready to hear Your gospel message and be saved. I love You, Lord. Amen.

Chapter 3

The Term Bible Was First Used B.C.

Those who have researched the word "Bible" would know that this term was first used around 223 AD. This is when a collection of the Old and New Testament books came together. Since this time, Christians have trusted the Bible as the inspired Word of God. Mormons challenge Christians by rejecting the principle of Sola Scriptura, which emphasizes the authority of the current scriptures alone. They believe that the Book of Mormon, Pearl of Great Price, and Doctrine and Covenants are also scripture. So they do not accept Sola Scriptura. Therefore, they call us foolish for thinking that all we need is the Bible. I've even had missionaries and other Mormons use different verses from their Book of Mormon to make their point. Here is one of those verses. It reads, "and because my words shall hiss forth—many of the Gentiles shall say: A Bible! A Bible! We have got a Bible, and there cannot be any more Bible." (2 Nephi 29:3) There is a big problem with this verse since the term "Bible" had not yet been coined yet.

Nobody had knowledge about the word "Bible" around 559 to 545 BC. This is the timeframe in 2 Nephi, chapter 29, which doesn't make sense. The term, "word of God" was around, but not the Bible. It is written, "every word of God is pure: he is a shield unto them that put their trust in him." (Proverbs 30:5) However, Joseph Smith didn't seem to care and wrote this about trusting in only the Bible. It is written, "thou fool, that shall say: A Bible, we have got a Bible, and we need no more Bible. Have ye obtained a Bible save it were by the Jews?" (2 Nephi 29:6) This is to make fun of Christians that rely on Sola Scriptura. Mormons would like to tell you that this is a prophecy about the Bible in the future. How people will say they don't need anything else but the Bible. However, this is simply an evil tactic put in the Book of Mormon by Joseph Smith. The more people that read these verses, the more people will think they need books outside the Bible.

When I was a Mormon, I would read these verses in 2 Nephi 29 and laugh at people who thought all they needed was the Bible. Thankfully, the Lord led me out in 2012. Oh, how things are different now. Truly, these two verses have caused Mormons to become so hard-hearted. Thankfully, there are still some people who are ready to receive the gospel message in the Bible. Speaking of the text, it says, "add thou not unto his words, lest he reprove thee, and thou be found a liar." (Proverbs 30:6) The Book of Mormon teaches that we should not trust the Bible alone. This can be seen in 2 Nephi 29. Therefore, Let's look at these verses in detail to find out why. It is written, "and because my words shall hiss forth—many of the Gentiles shall say: A Bible! A Bible! We have got a Bible, and there cannot be any more Bible." (2 Nephi 29:3) "thou fool, that shall say: A Bible, we have got a Bible, and we need no more Bible. Have ye obtained a Bible save it were by the Jews?" (2 Nephi 29:6)

The Bible was not around during this timeframe of the Book of Mormon, nor was this word known by people. It wasn't until 360 A.D., that the Bible was canonized and the term was first documented. Sure, Mormons like to use verses in their Book of Mormon to say they need extra-Biblical books. This is to counteract the Christian beliefs of Sola Scriptura. What they don't realize is that they have just proven their own precious book false in using them. Again, the term Bible was not used for centuries after these verses would have been written. What the Bible is, is a collection of books that were gathered during the canonization process. As for those books, "every word of God is pure: he is a shield unto them that put their trust in him." (Proverbs 30:5) Praise God! His Word has come together in the form of the Bible. In researching the term 'Bible,' I stumbled upon a website that provided the answers I needed when it comes to the Bible and how it came together. This is important to read and understand, for we learn that the Bible is a collection of Holy Spirit filled books.

The following is an excerpt about the canonization process. It reads, "the Council of Laodicea (360 AD), with the permission of the Pope in Rome, produced the first canon of the Bible. But it is only in the year of Pope Damasus (367 AD) a great effort was made to form a Bible. This Holy Pope compiled the books which he considered to be genuine and ordered St. Jerome to translate them into Latin, which was the official language of the Church. St. Jerome went to Jerusalem and lived 30 years in a cave to do the job. At 397 AD, he finished his works and presented it to the Pope. This is known as 'Latin Vulgate.' Pope Siricius called it the 'Bible,' which means 'collection of books.'" (Know The Catholic Truth) This information about the canon is very important, and we should trust it was compiled correctly. The truth is, Joseph Smith wanted people to trust in his book more so than the Bible. Talking to LDS people, they will even say that they trust the Bible as far as it is translated correctly. They would never say this about their Book of Mormon, although it has undergone many changes over the years. Amen.

Let us pray:

Oh Lord, help us make the right choices when the truth is presented to us. Our current lifestyle may feel quite comfortable. However, people are missing out on salvation when they disregard Your truths. It should not matter if people in our families stop talking to us because of our new faith in You, Jesus. You have said that some families have to be divided because of Your truth. I also feel like it is important to lead people out of their false beliefs. Some people think that if they were to leave their church, their spouse would leave them. So it is better to be married than to fight and get into a divorce. They say that You would never want to split up their family. Lord, why is it that people have made up a God to fit their own beliefs instead of getting Your truths from the Bible? Mormonism is one of these cults that have millions of people trapped in it. They cannot see it this way, but in reality, they are following man-made teachings that don't lead to heaven. Lord, You have led me to speak to hundreds of LDS people over these years. Many of them are LDS missionaries. I do not know all the fruit of these labors, but You do. I pray that many of them have renounced their false beliefs and come to You, Jesus, for salvation. I love You, Lord. Amen.

Chapter 4

Blacks Are Cursed

A contradiction in the Book of Mormon when compared to the Bible, comes from 2 Nephi, chapter 5. Reading the following verses will help you know how the God of Mormonism is racist. It is written, "wherefore, the word of the Lord was fulfilled which he spake unto me, saying that: Inasmuch as they will not hearken unto thy words they shall be cut off from the presence of the Lord. And behold, they were cut off from his presence. And he had caused the cursing to come upon them, yea, even a sore cursing, because of their iniquity. For behold, they had hardened their hearts against him, that they had become like unto a flint; wherefore, as they were white, and exceedingly fair and delightsome, that they might not be enticing unto my people the Lord God did cause a skin of blackness to come upon them. And thus saith the Lord God: I will cause that they shall be loathsome unto thy people, save they shall repent of their iniquities." (2 Nephi 5:20-22) So black people are wicked in God's sight?

The God of the Bible cares about our inner person and motives, unlike the racist God of Mormonism. He doesn't care about the outside appearance. He is not a respecter of persons. Every person of every race is important in his sight. It is written, "but the Lord said unto Samuel, Look not on his countenance, or on the height of his stature; because I have refused him: for the Lord seeth not as man seeth; for man looketh on the outward appearance, but the Lord looketh on the heart." (1 Samuel 16:7) "Then Peter opened his mouth, and said, Of a truth I perceive that God is no respecter of persons: But in every nation he that feareth him, and worketh righteousness, is accepted with him." (Acts 10:34,35) "There is neither Jew nor Greek, there is neither bond nor free, there is neither male nor female: for ye are all one in Christ Jesus." (Galatians 3:28) Surely, the God of the Bible is not racist, unlike the God of Mormonism. It is important to see the problems with racism in this book, as it is a contradiction to the Bible.

The God of the Bible has a no racism policy. He is a respecter of all people, no matter their skin color. However, the God of Mormonism is very racist. He even caused a skin of blackness to fall upon people who were wicked in the Book of Mormon. It was later on that the black people could return to being white if they repented of their sins. This is very sick and wrong. Black lives matter, just as all other skin colors do. It is written, "and the gospel of Jesus Christ shall be declared among them; wherefore, they shall be restored unto the knowledge of their fathers, and also to the knowledge of Jesus Christ, which was had among their fathers. And then shall they rejoice; for they shall know that it is a blessing unto them from the hand of God; and their scales of darkness shall begin to fall from their eyes; and many generations shall not pass away among them, save they shall be a pure and a delightsome people." (2 Nephi 30:5,6) This contradicts the Bible, but goes right along with what Joseph Smith taught as well about black people. The Bible says, "judge not according to the appearance, but judge righteous judgment." (John 7:24)

The Bible says that "there is neither Jew nor Greek, there is neither bond nor free, there is neither male nor female: for ye are all one in Christ Jesus." (Galatians 3:28) However, Mormonism started off with being racist. Joseph Smith said the following. It is written, "having learned with extreme regret, that an article entitled, Free People of Color; in the last number of the Star has been misunderstood, we feel in duty bound to state, in this Extra, that our intention was not only to stop free people of color from emigrating to this state, but to prevent them from being admitted as members of the church." (History of the Church, 1:378-379) "Had I anything to do with the negro, I would confine them by strict law to their own species and put them on a national equalization." (History of the Church, 5:218-219) Does this sound like someone who is a respecter of people of all colors? Absolutely, not. However, it makes sense that we have these racist undertones in their Book of Mormon also. The writer was racist, so it makes sense. This is in comparison to the Bible.

It is written, "but the Lord said unto Samuel, Look not on his coun-tenance, or on the height of his stature; because I have refused him: for the Lord seeth not as man seeth; for man looketh on the outward appearance, but the Lord looketh on the heart." (1 Samuel 16:7) So the God of the Bible doesn't look at the outside appearance, But what does the God of the Book of Mormon judge us on? This god punishes white people who sin against Him with black skin. This is a curse given to people who wrong Him. The same god of Mormonism is able to separate the righteous from the wicked depending upon their skin color. So white being righteous, and black being wicked. This is blasphemy! But what happens if someone repents and is black skinned? Their white skin would return to them like before. Does this sound like the same God of the Bible? Of course not. So how come people believe in the Book of Mormon when its contents are racist and the Bible is not?

Mormonism began with people who were racist, and their thinking made it into their Book of Mormon. The church may not be racist today, but what I see in their book still leaves a sour taste in my mouth. I see a racist god every time I read from the pages. But let's read for ourselves what the Book of Mormon says. "And the skins of the Lamanites were dark, according to the mark which was set upon their fathers, which was a curse upon them because of their transgression and their rebellion against their brethren, who consisted of Nephi, Jacob, and Joseph, and Sam, who were just and holy men." (Alma 3:6) As these people repented, "their curse was taken from them, and their skin became white like unto the Nephites." (3 Nephi 2:15) Does this sound racist? It sure does. Reading this makes me wonder why people of other races are part of this cult. Can they not see this dilemma?

The God of the Bible is not the same as the god of the Book of Mormon. We are told by Jesus to not judge according to the skin color of people. it is written, "judge not according to the appearance, but judge righteous judgment." (John 7:24) How God treats everyone equally no matter their skin color. "Then Peter opened his mouth, and said, Of a truth I perceive that God is no respecter of persons: But in every nation he that feareth him, and worketh righteousness, is accepted with him." (Acts 10:34-35) Skin color doesn't matter in the sight of God. We are all one in Christ, no matter what we look like. Paul said, "there is neither Jew nor Greek, there is neither bond nor free, there is neither male nor female: for ye are all one in Christ Jesus."

(Galatians 3:28) People who treat people differently because of their skin color are sinning in the sight of God. James also said, "but if ye have respect to persons, ye commit sin, and are convinced of the law as transgressors." (James 2:9) The true God of the Bible would never make someone become black or another skin color due to their sinful nature. This is outright racist.

The god in the Book of Mormon is so different from the God of the Bible. The Book of Mormon god says that those who are black are wicked, while those who are white are righteous. This sounds pretty racist to me. So why do Mormons like to write this off like it is not an issue? I am speaking of four different places in this book that says that God cursed the white skinned Lamanites with black skin. As they were once white and delightsome, they became dark and loathsome in this god's sight. But it gets worse. Every black person who repented and came back to him became white once again. You can read this here. "And it came to pass that those Lamanites who had united with the Nephites were numbered among the Nephites; And their curse was taken from them, and their skin became white like unto the Nephites; And their young men and their daughters became exceedingly fair, and they were numbered among the Nephites, and were called Nephites. And thus ended the thirteenth year." (3 Nephi 2:14-16) Again, would a true God change black people to be white skinned if they repented and came back to Him? Absolutely not. This is racist.

Let's talk about the one true God of Israel. Our God is the creator of every person on earth. And as the creator, He is the Father of our spirits. It is written, "and Moses spake unto the Lord, saying, let the Lord, the God of the spirits of all flesh, set a man over the congregation." (Numbers 27:15,16) This means that there is no prejudice with God. He even calls the human race very good in His sight. "And God said,

Let us make man in our image, after our likeness: and let them have dominion over the fish of the sea, and over the fowl of the air, and over the cattle, and over all the earth, and over every creeping thing that creepeth upon the earth. So God created man in his own image, in the image of God created he him; male and female created he them." (Genesis 1:26,27) "And God saw every thing that he had made, and, behold, it was very good. And the evening and the morning were the sixth day." (Genesis 1:31) This includes every person of every race and color. The color of our skin is insignificant in God's sight, for He looks upon the heart. The God of the Bible differs greatly from the god of the Book of Mormon.

Racism was prevalent among the early church leaders in Mormonism. This same prejudice towards blacks made it into the Book of Mormon. This is made evident as we read the quotes from the leaders at that time, including Joseph Smith. This needs to be brought to light, as the Church of Jesus Christ of Latter-Day Saints has a haunting racist past. Thankfully, these discriminatory beliefs towards black people do not exist today except for the passages in this book and previous books of the past. We will see how racism made it into their Book of Mormon. It was Joseph Smith who authored this book with the help of some of his associates. His racist quotes are below, along with a variety of prophets and apostles in their church...

Joseph Smith

"Having learned with extreme regret, that an article entitled, "Free People of Color; in the last number of the Star has been misunderstood, we feel in duty bound to state, in this Extra, that our intention was not only to stop free people of color from emigrating to this state,

but to prevent them from being admitted as members of the church."
(History of the Church, 1:378-379)

"Had I anything to do with the negro, I would confine them by strict law to their own species and put them on a national equalization." (History of the Church, 5:218-219)

Brigham Young

"We must believe in slavery. This colored race have been subjected to severe curses, which they have in their families and their classes and in their various capacities brought upon themselves. And until the curse is removed by Him who placed it upon them, they must suffer under its consequences; I am not authorized to remove it. I am a firm believer in slavery." (The Teachings of President Brigham Young, Volume 3: 1852-1854)

"You must not think, from what I say, that I am opposed to slavery. No! The negro is damned, and is to serve his master till God chooses to remove the curse of Ham." (New York Herald, May 4, 1855)

The First Presidency

"From the days of the Prophet Joseph even until now, it has been the doctrine of the church, never questioned by any of the Church leaders, that the Negroes are not entitled to the full blessings of the Gospel." (Letter from the First Presidency to Dr, Lowry Nelson, July 17, 1947)

"The attitude of the Church with reference to the Negroes remains as it has always stood. It is not a matter of the declaration of a policy but of direct commandment from the Lord, on which is founded the doctrine of the Church from the days of its organization, to the effect that Negroes may become members of the Church but that they are not entitled to the priesthood at the present time." (Statement of the First Presidency of the LDS Church, August 17, 1949)

Mark E. Petersen

"If that Negro is faithful all his days, he can and will enter the celestial kingdom. He will go there as a servant, but he will get a celestial resurrection. He will get a place in the celestial glory." Therefore, do Mormons consider God to have an "equal heaven" for all races?" (Speech at Brigham Young University on August 27 1954)

Bruce R. McConkie

"The negroes are not equal with other races where the receipt of certain spiritual blessings are concerned...But this inequality is not of man's origin. It is the Lord's doing." (1966 edition of Mormon Doctrine)

Racism in the Book of Mormon is evident from the attitudes of Joseph Smith and the church leaders during that time. You will notice while reading different verses that the racism in the 1800s ended up in the passages. The verses teach us that God punishes white people who sin against Him with black skin. This was a curse given to people who transgressed against Him. These people are then separated from the righteous because of their black skin. However, if they repented, their white skin would return to them like before. How racist is this? Does this sound like the God of the Bible? Absolutely not. See for yourself how racist the Mormon god really is by reading the different verses below...

"Wherefore, the word of the Lord was fulfilled which he spake unto me, saying that: Inasmuch as they will not hearken unto thy words they shall be cut off from the presence of the Lord. And behold, they were cut off from his presence. And he had caused the cursing to come upon them, yea, even a sore cursing, because of their iniquity. For behold, they had hardened their hearts against him, that they had become like unto a flint; wherefore, as they were white, and exceedingly fair and delightsome, that they might not be enticing unto my people the Lord God did cause a skin of blackness to come upon them. And thus saith the Lord God: I will cause that they shall be loathsome unto thy people, save they shall repent of their iniquities." (2 Nephi 5:20-22)

"And the gospel of Jesus Christ shall be declared among them; wherefore, they shall be restored unto the knowledge of their fathers, and also to the knowledge of Jesus Christ, which was had among their fathers. And then shall they rejoice; for they shall know that it is a blessing unto them from the hand of God; and their scales of darkness shall begin to fall from their eyes; and many generations shall not pass away among them, save they shall be a pure and a delightsome people." (2 Nephi 30:5,6)

"And the skins of the Lamanites were dark, according to the mark which was set upon their fathers, which was a curse upon them because of their transgression and their rebellion against their brethren, who consisted of Nephi, Jacob, and Joseph, and Sam, who were just and holy men." (Alma 3:6)

"And it came to pass that those Lamanites who had united with the Nephites were numbered among the Nephites; And their curse was taken from them, and their skin became white like unto the Nephites; And their young men and their daughters became exceedingly fair, and they were numbered among the Nephites, and were called Nephites. And thus ended the thirteenth year." (3 Nephi 2:14-16)

What does the Bible say about racism? Is the God of the Bible the same as what we read in the Book of Mormon? Absolutely not. God loves people of all skin colors equally and does not discriminate based on race. As you will see below, God does not differentiate people when it comes to their outward appearance. He already knows who is for Him and who is against Him. This is because all colors of skin are the same in his eyes.

This is in comparison to the Bible below:

"But the Lord said unto Samuel, Look not on his countenance, or on the height of his stature; because I have refused him: for the Lord seeth not as man seeth; for man looketh on the outward appearance, but the Lord looketh on the heart." (1 Samuel 16:7)

"Judge not according to the appearance, but judge righteous judgment." (John 7:24)

"Then Peter opened his mouth, and said, Of a truth I perceive that God is no respecter of persons: But in every nation he that feareth him, and worketh righteousness, is accepted with him." (Acts 10:34,35)

"For there is no respect of persons with God." (Romans 2:11)

"There is neither Jew nor Greek, there is neither bond nor free, there is neither male nor female: for ye are all one in Christ Jesus." (Galatians 3:28)

Here is the truth about racism. It was not part of God's church. So, seeing it in Mormonism makes me wonder why they claim to be the true church. Even if in 1978, racist slurs were removed, and blacks began to receive the priesthood, this doesn't change the past. What was said about blacks over a hundred and fifty years ago was still wrong. If I was a member of the church and I saw how racist it was, I would doubt that the church had any revelation from God. And if God was not leading them, I'd be finding a new church immediately. All this needs to be considered since the god they believe in said that blacks would never hold the priesthood. Did their god change his mind? The God of the Bible doesn't change his mind on what is sin, and who is cursed. People of every skin color deserve to be part of God's church, and also receive His blessings. Too bad this didn't happen in this church from the beginning. It claims to have the truth of God, but you can tell they are far from it. Please think about this.

The Book of Mormon is racist and not of God. Its racist slurs are from the pit of hell and uncalled-for. If I was part of this church, I would run as fast as I could in the opposite direction. Only then can Jesus save me. This is not something that people want to hear, but it must be said, nonetheless. Exposing the racism found in the Book of Mormon, and among the church leaders at the time, is not to judge this church wrongfully. This is making a righteous judgment call. Let me ask you a question. If you saw someone in a burning house, would you just allow them to suffer and die in it? I hope not. As for me, I would go into the house and pull them out of the flames. This is exactly what God has called all of us to do. Mormons are on the path of destruction and leading them off that path to Jesus is the least we can do. I do this out of love for every person in this false religion. If God has saved you from the pit of hell, praise God. The Lord Jesus is worthy of our praise. Thank Him this day for saving you, and for leading you on the path to heaven. Amen.

Let us pray:

Oh Lord, I pray that more people will be led by You and Your truth, and not the things people think are true. What we see in this world can appear to be good on the surface, especially certain beliefs. On paper, things can look very appealing and good for our families. Especially when it will impact us in this life and the next in a positive way. This is why I remain steadfast in prayer that You may show me the truth on a daily basis. Help us to be cognizant of the evils in this world and not dive into things without going to You first in prayer and Bible study. Investigating things that appear to be for You is the least I can do. Lest I fall into believing the doctrines of men. Help us follow You and not what our flesh wants. The times I get out of line is when I try to do my own things and not follow Your will. Often, I have fallen flat on my face when I am not seeking You. Therefore, I ask that You will lead me in all things. Keep me on Your righteous and holy path that leads to heaven. I am Yours and You are mine. I trust in You, Lord. I love You. Amen.

Chapter 5

Christians Were In The Church B.C.

In the Old Testament of the Bible, one would not find a single mention of the words "Church" or "Christian." This is because the church was not formed yet. During the times of the Old Covenant, the laws of Moses prevailed, where God's Tabernacle was on earth instead. However, if you were to look at the same time frames in the Book of Mormon, these words are present. It doesn't just exist in one chapter but many. Today we will look at Alma, chapter 46, where it makes mention of both "Church" and "Christian". This took place in 73 B.C, according to this chapter. The verses read, "for thus were all the true believers of Christ, who belonged to the church of God, called by those who did not belong to the church. And those who did belong to the church were faithful; yea, all those who were true believers in Christ took upon them, gladly, the name of Christ, or Christians as they were called, because of their belief in Christ who should come." (Alma 46:14,15) Can anybody spot the issue in these verses? The time frame is in the Old Covenant, so what happened here does not fit the timeline of the Bible.

The first mention of the word "Church" comes from Jesus. He mentioned that Peter would help lead it and that his church would never fail. It is written, "and I say also unto thee, That thou art Peter, and upon this rock I will build my church; and the gates of hell shall not prevail against it." (Matthew 16:18) Jesus used his disciples to help usher in His church on earth. This happened on the day of Pentecost, when the Holy Spirit was ushered in. These believers came "praising God, and having favor with all the people. And the Lord added to the church daily such as should be saved." (Acts 2:47) Notice how they were added to Christ's church. Speaking of these people, they were also called "Christians". "And when he had found him, he brought him unto Antioch. And it came to pass, that a whole year they assembled themselves with the church, and taught much people. And the disciples were called Christians first in Antioch." (Acts 11:26) The church was formed, and people were called Christians after Jesus's ascension into heaven.

People began to be called Christians starting in Acts, chapter 11. The gospel was preached to the Gentiles, and those who followed Jesus were called His disciples. A nickname given to the followers of Jesus is "Christians". This is the reason why we have Christianity in the world today. It is because it is made up of Christians and unbelievers. Those who are for Jesus and those who are against. This formation of Christ's church happened on the day of Pentecost, or A.D. 33. What we see in the Book of Mormon doesn't make sense. Things should have been very similar to the times in the Old Testament, but it isn't. We see Christ's church being formed before His birth. People were also being baptized as members of it. This should be cause for concern if you understand the timeline of the Bible. The Book of Mormon claims to have Christ's church formed in 73 B.C. This is not possible. As I've mentioned above, this contradiction leads readers to believe that the Book of Mormon is false. Don't read or trust it. Joseph Smith has already led millions of people astray through this book. Amen.

Let us pray:

Oh Lord, I pray that LDS people will wake up to the false teachings in their Book of Mormon. These people are so lost and don't even realize it. I want to reach them for Your cause, Jesus, but I am afraid that a lot of things I do will fall upon deaf ears. These people's hearts, minds, and ears are closed off to what Christians have to say. Only what is found in their cult do they acknowledge as truth. It is sad, God, that they reject messages that come from the Bible. The Book of Mormon teaches many false doctrines. One being, that Your church was set apart in the times of the laws of Moses or the old covenant times. The same goes with the word "Christians", being a part of their book also at that timeframe. Lord, how is it that people in Mormonism cannot see the issues here? I know for a fact that Your church began on the day of Pentecost. You poured out the Holy Spirit upon the earth and many people were saved that day. People gave their lives to You and were added to Your church. Lord, thank You for making Your teachings so clear. Only You could open my eyes to see the truth and set me free. I love You, Jesus. Amen.

Chapter 6

Church Was Formed B.C.

In the Book of Mormon, it describes how churches were being established in the Old Testament timeline. However, this is different than what we see in Israel around the same time period. We do not see churches in the Old Testament but synagogues. Jesus hadn't come to setup His church yet. As for Joseph's book, it speaks of churches before Jesus was born, and how the Gentiles were called apostates. They are treated as false teachers from false churches. It is written, "and it shall come to pass, that those who have dwindled in unbelief shall be smitten by the hand of the Gentiles. And the Gentiles are lifted up in the pride of their eyes, and have stumbled, because of the greatness of their stumbling block, that they have built up many churches; nevertheless, they put down the power and miracles of God, and preach up unto themselves their own wisdom and their own learning, that they may get gain and grind upon the face of the poor." (2 Nephi 26:19,20) This is how Joseph Smith saw churches in his timeframe. Not that churches existed in the Old Testament times.

The Bible teaches that anyone who is not Jewish is a gentile. This includes people from every religion minus those in Israel, including those in Mormonism. How interesting that this book attacks churches built up by Gentiles. Do they not realize they are Gentiles as well? What they don't realize is, millions of Gentiles have been saved in the last two thousand years because of their faith in Jesus. This teaching that Gentiles could receive Jesus and be saved was a mystery kept for centuries until the time of Paul. It is written, "how that by revelation he made known unto me the mystery; (as I wrote afore in few words, whereby, when ye read, ye may understand my knowledge in the mystery of Christ. Which in other ages was not made known unto the sons of men, as it is now revealed unto his holy apostles and prophets by the Spirit; That the Gentiles should be fellowheirs, and of the same body, and partakers of his promise in Christ by the gospel." (Ephesians 3:3-6) Therefore, every gentile who believes in Jesus is saved.

During the ministry of Jesus, He spoke about His church and how Peter would help bring it forth. Jesus is the rock on which the church stands. There was no church formed before this was mentioned. Jesus said, "and I say also unto thee, That thou art Peter, and upon this rock I will build my church; and the gates of hell shall not prevail against it." (Matthew 16:18). This is talking about the church forming through Christ and bringing it to pass on the day of Pentecost. The church was formed on this day just as Jesus spoke. It is written, "but Peter, standing up with the eleven, lifted up his voice, and said unto them, Ye men of Judaea, and all ye that dwell at Jerusalem, be this known unto you, and hearken to my words." (Acts 2:14) So Jesus started His church by way of the Holy Spirit. Peter and the apostles were leading the charge. The people were baptized and added to Christ's church on a daily basis. Speaking of those people, they were "praising

God, and having favour with all the people. And the Lord added to the church daily such as should be saved." (Acts 2:47) Therefore, the church began around 33 A.D.

The Book of Mormon tells a different story of when the church began. It says it happened around 147 B.C, not 33 A.D. as the Bible teaches. It is in this book that we learn about people who repented of their sins and came to the waters of baptism. A fictional character named Alma is seen baptizing different individuals. When coming out of the water, they receive the Holy Spirit. This is a contradiction to the Bible, as the Holy Spirit was not poured out until the day of Pentecost. The words of Joel were fulfilled on that special day. It is written, "and it shall come to pass in the last days, saith God, I will pour out of my Spirit upon all flesh." (Acts 2:17) This is in stark contrast to the people being baptized in 147 B.C, supposedly on the American Continent. It says these people were added to Christ's church first. It is written, "and they were called the church of God, or the church of Christ, from that time forward. And it came to pass that whosoever was baptized by the power and authority of God was added to his church." (Mosiah 18:17) And there you have it. The Church began around 33 A.D. On the day of Pentecost, and any other stories before this are false. This includes the churches being established before Christ's birth in the Book of Mormon.

Lastly, believers in Christ were called Christians in the Book of Mormon. This was supposedly around 72 B.C. It is written, "For thus were all the true believers of Christ, who belonged to the church of God, called by those who did not belong to the church. And those who did belong to the church were faithful; yea, all those who were true believers in Christ took upon them, gladly, the name of Christ, or Christians as they were called, because of their belief in Christ who should come. And therefore, at this time, Moroni prayed that the cause of the Christians, and the freedom of the land might be favored. " (Alma 46:14-16) This is in comparison to the Bible when the term Christian was first used in the times of Paul in the New Testament. It is written, "Then departed Barnabas to Tarsus, for to seek Saul: And when he had found him, he brought him unto Antioch. And it came to pass, that a whole year they assembled themselves with the church, and taught much people. And the disciples were called Christians first in Antioch." (Acts 11:25,26) The truth is, there was no church formed before Christ came to earth, and Christians are part of that church. Therefore, the storyline of the Book of Mormon doesn't make any sense.

Let us pray:

Oh Lord, I pray that people will see the errors in their Book of Mormon, while starting to question it. Truly, Satan is the one that instigated the writing of this false book those two hundred years ago. Joseph Smith fell victim to an angel of light, and now many people are going down with the ship with this false prophet. Lord, help these people come to the truth. Many people have already died and gone to hell, but this doesn't have to happen to people who are alive. God, lead these people to Christians who would help them know Your truths. May they leave the cult for Your sake only. Yes, God, I love the Mormon people, but I feel the need to expose them. Their core doctrines are of the devil, and it makes me sad to see them believe this way. Thank You for helping me come out of it. I was raised Mormon, but my open heart helped me learn from you and unlearn what is false. I was lost until You came into my life and saved me. I would still be a Mormon today if You did not open my eyes when it came to what the Bible says.

It is so clear now that Mormonism teaches another gospel that does not save. Help many of them know this also. I love You, Jesus. Amen.

Chapter 7

Different Jesus

The Book of Mormon showcases a different Jesus by way of his teachings. If this is the real Jesus, He would not contradict what is said in the Biblical text. For example, this false Christ said the following. "And whoso believeth in me, and is baptized, the same shall be saved; and they are they who shall inherit the kingdom of God. And whoso believeth not in me, and is not baptized, shall be damned." (3 Nephi 11:33,34) It is also written, "and verily I say unto you, that ye are they of whom I said: Other sheep I have which are not of this fold; them also I must bring, and they shall hear my voice; and there shall be one fold, and one shepherd. And they understood me not, for they supposed it had been the Gentiles; for they understood not that the Gentiles should be converted through their preaching. And they understood me not that I said they shall hear my voice; and they understood me not that the Gentiles should not at any time hear my voice—that I should not manifest myself unto them save it were by the Holy Ghost. But behold, ye have both heard my voice, and seen me; and ye are my sheep, and ye are numbered among those whom the Father hath given me." (3 Nephi 15:21-24)

Looking at the verses in 3 Nephi, chapter 11, the false Jesus is leaving out what He said to the people in Israel. How believing not in Him damns somebody, not being baptized, as the Jesus of the Book of Mormon taught. It is written, "He that believeth and is baptized shall be saved; but he that believeth not shall be damned." (Mark 16:16) Paul would also not go against Jesus when he said this about being saved by faith alone. It is written, "for by grace are ye saved through faith; and that not of yourselves: it is the gift of God: Not of works, lest any man should boast." (Ephesians 2:8,9) The true Jesus also said this about his sheep. It is written, "and other sheep I have, which are not of this fold: them also I must bring, and they shall hear my voice; and there shall be one fold, and one shepherd." (John 10:16) To bad the false Jesus said what he said before knowing what Paul said here. It is written, "for I would not, brethren, that ye should be ignorant of this mystery, lest ye should be wise in your own conceits; that blindness in part is happened to Israel, until the fulness of the Gentiles be come in." (Romans 11:25) Therefore, the Gentiles are the lost sheep, and the Book of Mormon Jesus is false.

It is official, an LDS prophet admitted to worshiping a different Jesus than that in Christianity. This is huge and should cause many Mormons to re-evaluate their faith, even resigning from Mormonism once and for all. It was in 1998, that their beloved prophet said the following. "In bearing testimony of Jesus Christ, President Hinckley spoke of those outside the Church who say Latter-day Saints 'do not believe in the traditional Christ.' 'No, I don't. The traditional Christ of whom they speak is not the Christ of whom I speak. For the Christ of whom I speak has been revealed in this the Dispensation of the

Fullness of Times. He together with His Father, appeared to the boy Joseph Smith in the year 1820, and when Joseph left the grove that day, he knew more of the nature of God than all the learned ministers of the gospel of the ages.'" (LDS Church News Week ending June 20, 1998, p. 7) As we read, it now seems obvious that in Mormonism they believe in a different Jesus. But it gets worse from here.

It is written, "the Church of Jesus Christ of Latter-day Saints proclaims that Jesus Christ is the Son of God in the most literal sense. The body in which He performed His mission in the flesh was sired by that same Holy Being we worship as God, our Eternal Father. Jesus was not the son of Joseph, nor was He begotten by the Holy Ghost (The Teachings of Ezra Taft Benson, p. 7. See also the Church News, December 18, 2004, p. 16) Because of this teaching, Mormons believe the Father has a body of flesh and bones like Jesus. But wouldn't this mean that He would have been physically with Mary before she conceived? If so, then physical intercourse with the Father appears to be the case, which is sick and wrong. What else would "overshadow" mean if the Father had a body and not a Spirit. We will look at this verses next. Thankfully, this is not the case, as the Trinity was on full display during her conception. We have the Father's Spirit, as well as the Holy Spirit, coming upon Mary, which allowed her to conceive Jesus.

There is only one way that Jesus could have been born. Mary had the presence of the Father, Son, and Holy Spirit, or something physical happening to her and the Father. As the Father is Spirit, we see the Trinity being the winning factor. Jesus's Spirit came inside of Mary's womb, and He began to have flesh. It was the Father who formed the son into a baby. It is written, "and the angel answered and said unto her, The Holy Ghost shall come upon thee, and the power of the

Highest shall overshadow thee: therefore also that holy thing which shall be born of thee shall be called the Son of God." (Luke 1:35) Therefore, the Jesus we learn of in Mormonism is not the same as we see in Christianity. Instead of Jesus always existing, He became God like His Father. He wasn't Spirit with His Father's Spirit before His birth, but was with His resurrected Father in heaven. Our Father in heaven has always been God with the Son and Holy Spirit. However, in Mormonism, He became a God like all other gods in Mormonism did before Him. This, as well as Jesus being said to be the brother of Lucifer, are damnable heresies taught by false teachers.

As mentioned, there are big problems in the way that Jesus is portrayed in Mormonism. These are just three examples, but there are more. Jesus is said to be the brother of Lucifer, instead of being His creator. His Father is said to have a body, not being a Spirit only. His atonement started in Gethsemane and ended on the cross, and not the cross alone. Paul warned us about false Christs. It is written, "for if he that cometh preacheth another Jesus, whom we have not preached, or if ye receive another spirit, which ye have not received, or another gospel, which ye have not accepted, ye might well bear with him." (2 Corinthians 11:4) Jesus created all things, including Lucifer. It is written, "for by him were all things created, that are in heaven, and that are in earth, visible and invisible, whether they be thrones, or dominions, or principalities, or powers: all things were created by him, and for him: And he is before all things, and by him all things consist." (Colossians 1:16,17)

Jesus taught that the Father is Spirit. It is written, "God is a Spirit: and they that worship him must worship him in spirit and in truth." (John 4:24) We know this since His Spirit dwells in the Son, like the Holy Spirit dwells in us. The Lord Jesus taught, "believest thou not that I am in the Father, and the Father in me? the words that I speak unto you I speak not of myself: but the Father that dwelleth in me, he doeth the works." (John 14:10) When Jesus died for our sins, this is when the atonement took place. It is written, "for if, when we were enemies, we were reconciled to God by the death of his Son, much more, being reconciled, we shall be saved by his life. And not only so, but we also joy in God through our Lord Jesus Christ, by whom we have now received the atonement." (Romans 5:10,11) Atonement took place with Jesus's death on the cross. The gospel message is that Jesus died for our sins, was buried, and rose from the grave. It does not include Gethsemane. To say it does is wrong. Believing a different Jesus is a salvation issue. If only Mormons could see this, while humbling themselves before God.

Believing in a different Jesus is a serious matter. It is cause for alarm since Gordan B. Hinkley said he didn't believe in the Traditional Jesus of Christianity. Hinkley's statement reveals the heresy centering around Jesus. It can't be overlooked. The Church of Jesus Christ of Latter-Day Saints claim to be Christ's one and only true church. Yet, Hinkley said he doesn't believe in the Traditional Jesus of Christianity. In other words, he doesn't believe in the Biblical Jesus. Such a denial of the Jesus taught in the Bible could disqualify him from eternal life. By saying that they don't believe in the Traditional Jesus of Christianity, they are fabricating their own form of Jesus. Unfortunately, He does not save. Anyone who says they believe in a different Jesus than in Christianity would earn the title of "False Teacher". Knowing this should cause many people to resign from the Mormon church. Paul even said, "for if he that cometh preacheth another Jesus, whom we have not preached, or if ye receive another spirit, which ye have not received, or another gospel, which ye have not accepted, ye might well bear with him." (2 Corinthians 11:4)

In the timeframe of the early church, there were many wolves. Those who deceived the sheep into believing in a different Jesus. So, what would the Mormon prophet be meaning by not believing in the traditional Jesus? It means that the Mormon Jesus is different. We see that in their teachings. How He is the brother of Lucifer, became a God like His Father, is a created being, his Father has a body of flesh and bones, He atoned for our sins in the garden, and did not create all things. As you can see, this Jesus is not the same Jesus of the Bible. Jesus is the creator of all thing's heaven and earth, including Lucifer. He has always existed and has always been God, like His Father. Our Father is a Spirit, and He sent His Son to die for our sins. Jesus then became flesh and atoned for our sins on the cross. Ask any Mormon, and they will admit that what I just said about their Jesus is correct. Therefore, these people simply bear with what is false, instead of running from it. If only their hearts were humble to come to the real Jesus of the Bible things would change. Amen.

Let us pray:

Oh Lord, seeing a false Jesus in Mormonism compels me to proclaim the truth loudly and passionately. But help me to do this with the help of the Holy Spirit. I am only one person. So prepare an army of believers to reach those who are lost for Your cause. May people's hearts be opened to Your truth. As hard as it is to reach them, I pray that a miracle will happen. I pray that the LDS missionaries will leave the mission fields to follow You. This has happened to people, and I am grateful that they had enough courage to do this. Even if there was much backlash and ridicule from their families when they got home, it was worth it. God, if I knew what I know now, I would have also done this and left my mission early while I was in the Mormon church. All I know is that You were preparing me for a time and space, in which

You could better use me for Your kingdom. Lord, I am grateful that You kept working on my heart, even though it took a while. You are so patient with me. Thank You, Lord, for saving a wretch like me. I love You, Jesus. Amen.

Chapter 8

The Father Is Spirit

In the Book of Mormon we learn that God is Spirit, not with flesh and bones, just like the Bible teaches. However, in the core teachings of Mormonism, the Father has a body of flesh and bones. He is like Jesus, having a glorified body. At a young age, they teach children in their church this false doctrine. In a lesson for kids, the teacher instructs the following. "To help each child understand that Heavenly Father is a real person, with a perfected body of flesh and bones, and that we are made in his image." (Heavenly Father has a body) But how do they explain away the following verses in their Book of Mormon? It is written, "and Ammon began to speak unto him with boldness, and said unto him: Believest thou that there is a God? And he answered, and said unto him: I do not know what that meaneth. And then Ammon said: Believest thou that there is a Great Spirit? And he said, Yea. And Ammon said: This is God. And Ammon said unto him again: Believest thou that this Great Spirit, who is God, created all things which are in heaven and in the earth? And he said: Yea, I believe that he created all things which are in the earth; but I do not know the heavens." (Alma 18:24-29)

God the Father is Spirit only. It is written, "Jesus saith unto her, Woman, believe me, the hour cometh, when ye shall neither in this mountain, nor yet at Jerusalem, worship the Father. Ye worship ye know not what: we know what we worship: for salvation is of the Jews. But the hour cometh, and now is, when the true worshippers shall worship the Father in spirit and in truth: for the Father seeketh such to worship him. God is a Spirit: and they that worship him must worship him in spirit and in truth." (John 4:21-24) It doesn't say that God the Father has a body with His Spirit, but a Spirt only. And as a Spirit only, He is also an invisible God. Paul said, "giving thanks unto the Father, which hath made us meet to be partakers of the inheritance of the saints in light: Who hath delivered us from the power of darkness, and hath translated us into the kingdom of his dear Son: In whom we have redemption through his blood, even the forgiveness of sins: Who is the image of the invisible God, the firstborn of every creature." (Colossians 1:12-15) Spiritual beings may look like they have a body like us, but still, they are Spirit only. This is why God can be at any place and at any time.

The Bible teaches that the Father is Spirit, not having a body with flesh and bones. Jesus said this three times, while the apostle Paul taught this as well. Jesus said, "behold my hands and my feet, that it is I myself: handle me, and see; for a spirit hath not flesh and bones, as ye see me have." (Luke 24:39) Therefore, a Spirit has no flesh and bones. "But the hour cometh, and now is, when the true worshippers shall worship the Father in spirit and in truth: for the Father seeketh such to worship him. God is a Spirit: and they that worship him must worship him in spirit and in truth." (John 4:23,24) The Father is Spirit, and we worship Him in spirit and truth. "Believest thou not that I am in the Father, and the Father in me? the words that I speak unto you I speak not of myself: but the Father that dwelleth in me, he doeth the works." (John 14:8-10) The Father's Spirit is able to dwell in Jesus. Lastly, Paul said, "in whom we have redemption through his blood, even the forgiveness of sins: Who is the image of the invisible God, the firstborn of every creature." (Colossians 1:14,15) Being Spirit, the Father is also invisible to people on earth to see.

Joseph Smith, the founder of Mormonism, once taught that the Father is Spirit. How He does not have a physical body like the Son. You can see this taught in the "Lectures Of Faith" publication. He said the following...

"In our former lectures we treated of the being, character, perfections, and attributes of God. What we mean by perfections is, the perfections which belong to all the attributes of his nature. We shall in this lecture speak of the Godhead; we mean the Father, Son, and Holy Spirit. There are two personages who constitute the great, matchless, governing, and supreme power over all things – by whom all things were created and made that are created and made, whether visible or invisible; whether in heaven, on earth, or in the earth, under the earth, or throughout the immensity of space. They are the Father and the Son: The Father being a personage of spirit, glory, and power, possessing all perfection and fullness. The Son, who was in the bosom of the Father, a personage of tabernacle, made or fashioned like unto man, or being in the form and likeness of man – or rather, man was formed after his likeness and in his image. He is also the express image and likeness of the personage of the Father, possessing all the fullness of the Father, or the same fullness with the Father, being begotten of him; and was ordained from before the foundation of the world to be a propitiation for the sins of all those who should believe on his name; and is called the Son because of the flesh." (Lecture Of Faith, Section 5)

In Joseph's own book, the Book of Mormon, it teaches that the Father is Spirit. This goes right along with what Joseph Smith originally taught. These verses read...

"And Ammon began to speak unto him with boldness, and said unto him: Believest thou that there is a God? And he answered, and said unto him: I do not know what that meaneth. And then Ammon said: Believest thou that there is a Great Spirit? And he said, Yea. And Ammon said: This is God. And Ammon said unto him again: Believest thou that this Great Spirit, who is God, created all things which are in heaven and in the earth? And he said: Yea, I believe that he created all things which are in the earth; but I do not know the heavens." (Alma 18:24-29)

"And the king said: Is God that Great Spirit that brought our fathers out of the land of Jerusalem? And Aaron said unto him: Yea, he is that Great Spirit, and he created all things both in heaven and in earth. Believest thou this? And he said: Yea, I believe that the Great Spirit created all things, and I desire that ye should tell me concerning all these things, and I will believe thy words." (Alma 22:9-11)

This is where the tide turns in Mormonism. Near the end of Joseph Smith's ministry on earth, his opinion changed. In his latest declaration, he stated that the Father has a body of flesh and bones like we have. You can find this teaching in Doctrine and Covenants. It reads...

"The Father has a body of flesh and bones as tangible as man's; the Son also; but the Holy Ghost has not a body of flesh and bones, but is a personage of Spirit. Were it not so, the Holy Ghost could not dwell in us." (Doctrine and Covenants 130:22)

It is interesting that Mormons believe that the Father has a physical body and not just Spirit. In the Book of Mormon, we learn that the Father is Spirit with no mention of a body. This can be found in Alma, chapters 18 and 22. It is in Doctrine and Covenants 130:22 that things change, which has caused the LDS people to believe that the Father has a body. How interesting that the verse says that the Holy Spirit dwells in us, making Him Spirit, but they don't realize that the Father dwells in the Son. Wouldn't the Father also be Spirit if He dwells in the Son, like the Holy Spirit dwells in us? Jesus said, "believest thou not that I am in the Father, and the Father in me? the words that I speak unto you I speak not of myself: but the Father that dwelleth in me, he doeth the works." (John 14:10) This makes sense, since Jesus became flesh, and not the Father. Jesus and the Father were once only Spirits. Jesus came down and became flesh. He died for our sins and rose to a glorified body in heaven.

Jesus said the Father is a spirit, for He dwells in Him, the same way the Holy Spirit dwells in us. As the Father dwells in the Son, he also does not have a body. Jesus said, "woman, believe me, the hour cometh, when ye shall neither in this mountain, nor yet at Jerusalem, worship the Father. Ye worship ye know not what: we know what we worship: for salvation is of the Jews. But the hour cometh, and now is, when the true worshippers shall worship the Father in spirit and in truth: for the Father seeketh such to worship him. God is a Spirit: and they that worship him must worship him in spirit and in truth." (John 4:21-24) He also taught that spirits do not have a body of flesh and bones. This means that our Father in heaven is Spirit only. It is written, "and as they thus spake, Jesus himself stood in the midst of them, and saith unto them, Peace be unto you. But they were terrified and affrighted, and supposed that they had seen a spirit. And he said unto them, Why are ye troubled? and why do thoughts arise in your hearts? Behold my hands and my feet, that it is I myself: handle me, and see; for a spirit hath not flesh and bones, as ye see me have." (Luke 24:36-39)

Either the Spirit of God dwells in us or He doesn't. We cannot have it both ways. Thankfully, we have the Biblical text that agree that God dwells in those who believe in Him. And not only this, we know that the Father dwells in the Son also. This is how God the Father can be in more than one place at once. God is not limited by time or space like humans because He is everywhere, being omnipresent. This is because, as Jesus said, spirits do not have flesh and bones as he has. Jesus even said that his Father is spirit, and we are to worship Him in spirit and in truth. For this reason, God is able to hear our prayers when we call upon His Name. This happens in any place all around the world. When you pray and sense God's presence, it means that God is with you, uplifting you and providing you with the hope and peace to continue on. This is true since God is omnipresent. It is important to let the Bible speak when it comes to this topic. See the following teachings about God the Father being spirit and how this is possible...

If you are a spirit, then you don't have flesh and bones.

"And he said unto them, Why are ye troubled? and why do thoughts arise in your hearts? Behold my hands and my feet, that it is I myself: handle me, and see; for a spirit hath not flesh and bones, as ye see me have." (Luke 24:38,39)

God the Father is spirit.

"But the hour cometh, and now is, when the true worshippers shall worship the Father in spirit and in truth: for the Father seeketh such to worship him. God is a Spirit: and they that worship him must worship him in spirit and in truth." (John 4:23,24)

The spirit of God dwells in the Son, as God the Father is spirit.

"And after this manner shall ye baptize in my name; for behold, verily I say unto you, that the Father, and the Son, and the Holy Ghost are one; and I am in the Father, and the Father in me, and the Father and I are one." (3 Nephi 11:27)

"Believest thou not that I am in the Father, and the Father in me? the words that I speak unto you I speak not of myself: but the Father that dwelleth in me, he doeth the works." (John 14:10)

The spirit of God dwells in us, not in temples made with hands.

"God that made the world and all things therein, seeing that he is Lord of heaven and earth, dwelleth not in temples made with hands; Neither is worshipped with men's hands, as though he needed any thing, seeing he giveth to all life, and breath, and all things; And hath made of one blood all nations of men for to dwell on all the face of the earth, and hath determined the times before appointed, and the bounds of their habitation." (Acts 17:24-26)

As we read in the verses above, the Bible does not contradict itself when it teaches that God the Father is spirit. The Book of Mormon disagrees with the official Mormon doctrine regarding God the Father having a physical body. Instead, it teaches that God's spirit is able to dwell in our hearts. This is not possible if the Father has a body of flesh and bones. LDS Doctrines have limited God's ability to be omnipresent. Seeing that they believe he has a physical body, this changes everything. It tells me that they are anti the true God of the Bible and not for Him. If you think that this is not a salvific issue, then you are wrong. Mormons teach and promote a false god that is made up of flesh and bones. This god does not save anyone. Therefore, salvation does not come through Mormonism. They have denied what Jesus taught about spirits not having flesh and bones. The worst part is that they deny that the Father is spirit. Lastly, see below how the Book of Mormon contradicts the Doctrine and Covenants...

The spirit of God dwells in us.

"And this I know, because the Lord hath said he dwelleth not in unholy temples, but in the hearts of the righteous doth he dwell; yea, and he has also said that the righteous shall sit down in his kingdom, to go no more out; but their garments should be made white through the blood of the Lamb." (Alma 34:36)

God is unable to dwell in us, for He has a body of flesh and bones.

"the Father has a body of flesh and bones as tangible as man's; the Son also; but the Holy Ghost has not a body of flesh and bones, but is a personage of Spirit. Were it not so, the Holy Ghost could not dwell in us." (Doctrine and Covenants 130:22)

So, who will you believe? Christianity and the Bible alone, or what Mormonism teaches? Where in the Mormon church, the Father could have a body or Spirit only? The spirit of truth is in the Bible, whereas the spirit of confusion is in Mormonism. If I were you, and were in the LDS church, I would leave it behind. Do this once and for all. Don't allow people to run your life with their extra laws, rules, regulations, covenants, and ordinances. Instead, allow God to govern

Your life the right way. It doesn't have to be complicated. What the Bible teaches is for today, as it has been for every generation. God's Word is His love letter left for mankind.

Lastly, Jesus became flesh and dwelt among us. He was Spirit before gaining a body of flesh and bones. As the Father was never born, He remains Spirit. As for the denomination we are part of, it does not matter. Never say that only your church is true, for this is a false statement. The Spirit of God dwells in the hearts of every believer, of many different Bible-believing churches all throughout the world. It doesn't matter what skin color a person has. God looks upon the heart and knows if we are for or against Him. This world is dark and going in the wrong direction, so decide today to worship the Father in spirit and truth. True worshipers do this while giving into His wisdom and knowledge for their lives. We are different in Christ Jesus, having been reborn in the spirit with God's Spirit. God bless you! Keep seeking Jesus daily, while reading the Bible and praying often. Amen.

Let us pray:

Oh Lord, thank You for teaching us that the Father is Spirit. Your Word speaks and says God's Spirit dwells in You, Jesus, which makes Him Spirit. I love to think about this in the same fashion as the Holy Spirit dwells in us, Your true believers. This analogy helps me relay this truth to the Mormon people. If only they would have a heart to listen, then the truth could come to light in their lives also. You taught that we worship the Father, for He is Spirit. How a Spirit does not have a body of flesh and bones as You have. Truly, you are my teacher, not the teachers of men. The false prophets in Mormonism need to be stopped. They are telling people that You have a body, Father, which causes confusion among Your people. If only they knew how false this teaching really is, then people would come to You and be saved. I believe in You, Jesus. I trust in You, God. Amen.

Chapter 9

Gentiles Are Not The Lost Sheep

In John, chapter 10, in the Bible, Jesus speaks of other sheep that are not part of Israel. He said, "and other sheep I have, which are not of this fold: them also I must bring, and they shall hear my voice; and there shall be one fold, and one shepherd." (John 10:16) As Christians, we understand that this references the Gentiles, who would later be adopted in through faith in Jesus. However, in 3 Nephi, chapter 15, it refers to the people in America instead. It reads, "and verily I say unto you, that ye are they of whom I said: Other sheep I have which are not of this fold; them also I must bring, and they shall hear my voice; and there shall be one fold, and one shepherd. And they understood me not, for they supposed it had been the Gentiles; for they understood not that the Gentiles should be converted through their preaching. And they understood me not that I said they shall hear my voice; and they understood me not that the Gentiles should not at any time hear my voice—that I should not manifest myself unto them save it were by the Holy Ghost. But behold, ye have both heard my voice, and seen me; and ye are my sheep, and ye are numbered among those whom the Father hath given me." (3 Nephi 15:21-24)

Looking at what you just read very closely, we see that the Gentiles are not the other sheep. But is this true? It is now time to uncover who the other sheep are according to the Biblical text. To understand this, let's look at John, chapter 10 once again. It reads, "I am the good shepherd, and know my sheep, and am known of mine. As the Father knoweth me, even so know I the Father: and I lay down my life for the sheep." (John 10:14,15) These verses come before the one we read earlier. The Lord's sheep are His people, which in verse 16 we learn that other people would later be grafted into the same fold as the Jews. This is explained in detail by Paul the apostle. It is written, "whereby, when ye read, ye may understand my knowledge in the mystery of Christ) Which in other ages was not made known unto the sons of men, as it is now revealed unto his holy apostles and prophets by the Spirit; That the Gentiles should be fellowheirs, and of the same body, and partakers of his promise in Christ by the gospel." (Ephesians 3:4-6) "For I would not, brethren, that ye should be ignorant of this mystery, lest ye should be wise in your own conceits; that blindness in part is happened to Israel, until the fulness of the Gentiles be come in." (Romans 11:25)

God's sheep are the people of Israel, and the other sheep that came in later are the Gentiles. The gospel is now for the Gentiles. Praise God that we, though we are not part of Israel, are grafted in. This is what the Bible teaches, and I also taught this when I was on an LDS mission. I believed that the "other sheep" were those who were not part of the fold of Christ. That God allows people into His fold through faith in Jesus. I would recite this verse all the time. "And other sheep I have, which are not of this fold: them also I must bring, and they shall hear my voice; and there shall be one fold, and one shepherd." (John 10:16) Even in Mormonism, I believed that those who were lost and without Jesus were the lost sheep, or the Gentiles. I did not subscribe to the people in America as these other sheep. I disagree with the statement in the Book of Mormon where it teaches that the Nephites, not the Gentiles, are his lost sheep. So even before my mission, I doubted these words in the Book of Mormon. This prepared me to be where I am today as a Christian. Now, let us look at the verses in 3 Nephi, chapter 15, again.

It is written, "and verily I say unto you, that ye are they of whom I said: Other sheep I have which are not of this fold; them also I must bring, and they shall hear my voice; and there shall be one fold, and one shepherd. And they understood me not, for they supposed it had been the Gentiles; for they understood not that the Gentiles should be converted through their preaching. And they understood me not that I said they shall hear my voice; and they understood me not that the Gentiles should not at any time hear my voice—that I should not manifest myself unto them save it were by the Holy Ghost. But behold, ye have both heard my voice, and seen me; and ye are my sheep, and ye are numbered among those whom the Father hath given me." (3 Nephi 15:21-24) The Jesus of the Bible is not speaking here. Joseph Smith made this part up about the Nephite people. it is sad that he attributed Jesus to his writing.

The question is, would Jesus ever contradict what His own apostles would later teach? Absolutely not. Now to make my point very clear, let's reexamine what Paul taught the people in Ephesus. It is written, "whereby, when ye read, ye may understand my knowledge in the mystery of Christ) Which in other ages was not made known unto the sons of men, as it is now revealed unto his holy apostles and prophets by the Spirit; That the Gentiles should be fellowheirs, and of the same body, and partakers of his promise in Christ by the gospel." (Ephesians 3:4-6) What else could the other sheep refer to but the Gentiles according to these verses? Were the Gentiles part of the same body of Israel? They were not. However, they are called sheep nonetheless, and are now fellow heirs, having been adopted through faith in Jesus. Reemphasizing what Paul taught the Romans, we will read that portion again also. "For I would not, brethren, that ye should be ignorant of this mystery, lest ye should be wise in your own conceits; that blindness in part is happened to Israel, until the fulness of the Gentiles be come in." (Romans 11:25) This is wonderful news. God is so loving as to allow us into His fold. Amen.

Let us pray:

Oh Lord, help every person who is lost and without a shepherd. We were once a far off, not being part of Your fold. Israel is your people, and I am so grateful to be adopted in. We stood looking in, wondering when we could be partakers also. Many people have believed in You, God, but they were unsure if they would be accepted due to restrictions against them. This must have been difficult for people to bear. Thankfully, You came down to save us, Jesus. We were always Your lost sheep, but now You have ushered us in. Thank You for trusting us. Those who would put their faith in You, Jesus. The tides have turned over the centuries, it seems. Israel has rejected You, Jesus, while the Gentiles have accepted You as their Lord, God, and King. You have not forgotten Israel but allow us to be a shining light in the darkness. You've sent us to bear witness Your truths in all the world. Help us, Lord, to be Your light in the darkness. There are many people searching for truth, but we need the Holy Spirit to do the talking. I love You, Jesus. I believe in You. Amen.

Chapter 10

Giftings Of the Holy Spirit B.C.

"Now concerning spiritual gifts, brethren, I would not have you ignorant. Ye know that ye were Gentiles, carried away unto these dumb idols, even as ye were led. Wherefore I give you to understand, that no man speaking by the Spirit of God calleth Jesus accursed: and that no man can say that Jesus is the Lord, but by the Holy Ghost. Now there are diversities of gifts, but the same Spirit. And there are differences of administrations, but the same Lord. And there are diversities of operations, but it is the same God which worketh all in all. But the manifestation of the Spirit is given to every man to profit withal. For to one is given by the Spirit the word of wisdom; to another the word of knowledge by the same Spirit; To another faith by the same Spirit; to another the gifts of healing by the same Spirit; To another the working of miracles; to another prophecy; to another discerning of spirits; to another divers kinds of tongues; to another the interpretation of tongues: But all these worketh that one and the selfsame Spirit, dividing to every man severally as he will." (1 Corinthians 12:1-11)

There are spiritual gifts given to different people in the church. Although we are many members of Christ's body, He bestows the best gifts upon each of us. These are the gifts from God unto His people on earth. Jesus had been desirous to give us these gifts, but they were unneeded until He ascended into heaven. This is because the comforter would be the one to fill us and bestow us God's spiritual giftings. Jesus said this about the power of the Holy Spirit in us. It is written, "and he said unto them, It is not for you to know the times or the seasons, which the Father hath put in his own power. But ye shall receive power, after that the Holy Ghost is come upon you: and ye shall be witnesses unto me both in Jerusalem, and in all Judaea, and in Samaria, and unto the uttermost part of the earth." (Acts 1:7,8) People who believe in the Lord Jesus Christ for salvation are given different giftings of the Spirit. Some people have the gift of healing, prophecy, tongues, and more. We don't see these gifts spoken of in times past, like in the Old Testament. The giftings of the Spirit were for Christ's church and in the future.

The Holy Ghost was bestowed upon the disciples of Jesus, and then thousands of others, on the day of Pentecost. It was approximately 33 A.D. at that time. However, the Book of Mormon says that we got this wrong. It teaches us that the outpouring of the Holy Spirit happened in the times of the old covenant. This would be around 559 B.C. See for yourself in the following verses in the Book of Mormon. "And also, the voice of the Son came unto me, saying: He that is baptized in my name, to him will the Father give the Holy Ghost, like unto me; wherefore, follow me, and do the things which ye have seen me do. Wherefore, my beloved brethren, I know that if ye shall follow the Son, with full purpose of heart, acting no hypocrisy and no deception before God, but with real intent, repenting of your sins, witnessing unto the Father that ye are willing to take upon you the name of Christ, by baptism—yea, by following your Lord and your Savior down into the water, according to his word, behold, then shall ye receive the Holy Ghost; yea, then cometh the baptism of fire and of the Holy Ghost; and then can ye speak with the tongue of angels, and shout praises unto the Holy One of Israel." (2 Nephi 31:12,13)

With the verses in 2 Nephi, chapter 31, Joseph Smith has removed the importance of the Holy Spirit on the day of Pentecost. We see this as the people of Nephi experienced this outpouring of the Holy Spirit 600 years beforehand. It is Satan that loves to take away the importance of different events in the Bible. Jesus promised us that this power would come after He ascended into heaven, not before. "And ye are witnesses of these things. And, behold, I send the promise of my Father upon you: but tarry ye in the city of Jerusalem, until ye be endued with power from on high." (Luke 24:48,49) And this happened just as the Lord said. "And when the day of Pentecost was fully come, they were all with one accord in one place. And suddenly there came a sound from heaven as of a rushing mighty wind, and it filled all the house where they were sitting. And there appeared unto them cloven tongues like fire, and it sat upon each of them. And they were all filled with the Holy Ghost, and began to speak with other tongues, as the Spirit gave them utterance." (Acts 2:1-4) In summary, the events in the Book of Mormon were fabricated. Joseph Smith and his friends authored this fictional story. Amen.

Let us pray:

Oh Lord, I pray that many people in the Mormon community will stop reading the Book of Mormon. I pray that they would get rid of it and start reading the Bible instead. Thank You for teaching me that all evil things must be removed from our lives. This includes this fictional and destructive Book of Mormon. It is such a wonderful feeling, just knowing that the things in our old lives are now gone. I am speaking of things that take us away from You, and cause us to believe in false doctrines, and so much more. Lord, You have shown me how evil the Mormon church is in general. I am willing to expose it in order to lead many of them to You for salvation. I am saddened to think that Joseph Smith has led millions of Mormons astray. People have idolized him and trusted in his false teachings instead of having faith in the Bible. God, these people's hearts are so hard-hearted. If only they knew the destructive path that is ahead of them, things would be different. Wake them up from their slumber. I pray that many of them will resign from their cult and come to You for salvation. I believe in You, Jesus. I love You. Amen.

Chapter 11

God Is Unchangeable

Concerning the Book of Mormon, Joseph Smith said, "I told the brethren that the Book of Mormon was the most correct of any book on earth, and the keystone of our religion, and a man would get nearer to God by abiding by its precepts, than by any other book." (The Introduction To The Book Of Mormon) This is a bold statement, as he is taking away from the importance of the Bible. Therefore, we will examine this book's teachings on God to see if the members of their church prescribe to them. There are four core teachings about God that Mormons would disagree with, but are taught in the Book of Mormon. 1. There is one God, and He is the Father, Son, and Holy Spirit. They are three persons in one being, thus the Holy Trinity. 2. There is only one God. 3. God never changes. 4. And that God has always been God and has always existed. These teachings are also taught in the Bible. However, when telling the members of the Mormon church about these truths, they reject them. The four truths I just mentioned are found in the Book of Mormon below...

The Book of Mormon teaches the following....

1. The Trinity. How the Father, the Son, and the Holy Spirit are one God.

"And now, behold, my beloved brethren, this is the way; and there is none other way nor name given under heaven whereby man can be saved in the kingdom of God. And now, behold, this is the doctrine of Christ, and the only and true doctrine of the Father, and of the Son, and of the Holy Ghost, which is one God, without end. Amen." (2 Nephi 31:21)

2. Only one God.

"And Zeezrom said unto him: Thou sayest there is a true and living God? And Amulek said: Yea, there is a true and living God. Now Zeezrom said: Is there more than one God? And he answered, No." (Alma 11:26-29)

3. God never changes.

"For do we not read that God is the same yesterday, today, and forever, and in him there is no variableness neither shadow of changing? And now, if ye have imagined up unto yourselves a god who doth vary, and in whom there is shadow of changing, then have ye imagined up unto yourselves a god who is not a God of miracles. But behold, I will show unto you a God of miracles, even the God of Abraham, and the God of Isaac, and the God of Jacob; and it is that same God who created the heavens and the earth, and all things that in them are." (Mormon 9:9-11)

"And who shall say that Jesus Christ did not do many mighty miracles? And there were many mighty miracles wrought by the hands of the apostles. And if there were miracles wrought then, why has God ceased to be a God of miracles and yet be an unchangeable Being? And behold, I say unto you he changeth not; if so he would cease to be God; and he ceaseth not to be God, and is a God of miracles." (Mormon 9:18,19)

4. God has always been God and has always existed.

"And now I come to that faith, of which I said I would speak; and I will tell you the way whereby ye may lay hold on every good thing. For behold, God knowing all things, being from everlasting to everlasting, behold, he sent angels to minister unto the children of men, to make manifest concerning the coming of Christ; and in Christ there should come every good thing." (Moroni 7:21,22)

"For I know that God is not a partial God, neither a changeable being; but he is unchangeable from all eternity to all eternity." (Moroni 8:18)

LDS people disagree with those verses and teach that there are three Gods in the godhead. There are not three persons in one God as the Book of Mormon teaches. Instead, they believe in a plurality of Gods in the heavens above. This is not including people who will be exalted as Gods themselves. They believe this happens in the highest heaven, called the Celestial glory. That the Father was not always God, but was once a man like we are now. Because He lived his life for God, He was exalted to Godhood in His resurrection. Joseph Smith taught, "I will go back to the beginning before the world was, to show what kind of being God is. What sort of being was God in the beginning? God himself was once as we are now, and is an exalted man, and sits enthroned in yonder heavens!" (Teachings Of The Prophet Joseph Smith pg.345) This sounds like a changeable God to me. The Bible and the Book of Mormon teach that God is eternal. He has always existed as God from the beginning to the end. It is interesting that

Mormonism teaches the opposite. That the Father was not always God.

As for the Bible, we also learn the following truths. That 1. There is one Father, one Son, and one Holy Spirit. They make up one God, thus the Trinity. "For there are three that bear record in heaven, the Father, the Word, and the Holy Ghost: and these three are one." (1 John 5:7) 2. How there is only one God. "Thus saith the Lord the King of Israel, and his redeemer the Lord of hosts; I am the first, and I am the last; and beside me there is no God." (Isaiah 44:6) 3. That God never changes. "For I am the Lord, I change not; therefore ye sons of Jacob are not consumed." (Malachi 3:6) 4. And that God has always been God and has always existed. "Before the mountains were brought forth, or ever thou hadst formed the earth and the world, even from everlasting to everlasting, thou art God." (Psalm 90:2) So yes, these verses in the Book of Mormon complement what the Bible says. However, this does not make the Book of Mormon true. Simply put, Joseph Smith once believed in certain parts of the Bible and wrote them in his book. What is interesting is that the members of his church do not believe in the verses I quoted. They say we are adding to the text of their Book of Mormon.

A question Mormons need to think about is this. Has God always been God? Is he unchangeable, or was he exalted to Godhood? Their Book of Mormon states that God has always existed. It reads, "for do we not read that God is the same yesterday, today, and forever, and in him there is no variableness neither shadow of changing?" (Mormon 9:9) "And if there were miracles wrought then, why has God ceased to be a God of miracles and yet be an unchangeable Being? And behold, I say unto you he changeth not; if so he would cease to be God; and he ceaseth not to be God, and is a God of miracles." (Mormon 9:19)

However, Joseph Smith taught something entirely different, which would make God to cease according to the Book of Mormon. How God was a man, being exalted to Godhood. He wrote, "God himself was once as we are now, and is an exalted man, and sits enthroned in yonder heavens! That is the great secret. If the veil were rent today, and the great God who holds this world in its orbit, and who upholds all worlds and all things by his power, was to make himself visible." (The King Follett Discourse) If I read this correctly, God was a man, being exalted to Godhood.

Thankfully, we have the Bible, and it teaches us about God always existing. Our Lord and God is from everlasting to everlasting. He is from the beginning and will continue forevermore. David wrote, "Lord, thou hast been our dwelling place in all generations. Before the mountains were brought forth, or ever thou hadst formed the earth and the world, even from everlasting to everlasting, thou art God." (Psalm 90:1,2) Jesus is that God, of whom the Father has always been with. Out of the mouth of Jesus Christ, the Prince of Peace, He said, "and he that sat upon the throne said, Behold, I make all things new. And he said unto me, Write: for these words are true and faithful. And he said unto me, It is done. I am Alpha and Omega, the beginning and the end. I will give unto him that is athirst of the fountain of the water of life freely." (Revelation 21:5,6) To be called the beginning and the end makes exaltation to Godhood impossible. Therefore, I urge all members of the "Church of Jesus Christ of Latter-Day Saints" to renounce this false belief of attaining godhood. There is only one God and He is from the beginning of time.

Another verse we can bring up to the Mormons comes from Moroni, chapter 8. It teaches that God has always existed and has never changed. He was not an exalted man to Godhood but has been God from all eternity. He was and is God. It reads, "for I know that God is not a partial God, neither a changeable being; but he is unchangeable from all eternity to all eternity." (Moroni 8:18) This is a teaching that Christians agree with, but Mormons do not. How interesting that they say the Book of Mormon is the most correct book on earth, but don't believe in many of the teachings. Even the author of this book, Joseph Smith, went against what he wrote about while teaching the exact opposite. Let's look at the portion of the quote that is the most damning. He said, "God himself was once as we are now, and is an exalted man, and sits enthroned in yonder heavens!" (The King Follett Discourse) I will admit that most of the Mormon people are not aware of this quote. Many Mormon missionaries are, but the LDS people are not always privy to this information. Therefore, the belief about God being an exalted man isn't accepted by everyone in that church. Thankfully, there are many that still believes that God has existed from time and all eternity. How He is the first and the last.

Exaltation for people to Godhood is not what the Book of Mormon teaches, nor what the Bible teaches either. Therefore, Mormons should be careful believing this doctrine. The one true God of the heavens has spoken and said, "thus saith the Lord the King of Israel, and his redeemer the Lord of hosts; I am the first, and I am the last; and beside me there is no God. And who, as I, shall call, and shall declare it, and set it in order for me, since I appointed the ancient people? and the things that are coming, and shall come, let them shew unto them. Fear ye not, neither be afraid: have not I told thee from that time, and have declared it? ye are even my witnesses. Is there a God beside me? yea, there is no God; I know not any." (Isaiah 44:6-8) To be called the first and the last means that there are no Gods beside Him. This puts a wrench into the doctrines of exaltations to Godhood. As explained, the one true God of the heavens has always existed. Jesus said, "I am Alpha and Omega, the beginning and the end, the first and the last." (Revelation 22:13) The God we worship as Christians knows of no other Gods. If He knows of no other Gods, then we will never reach Godhood. Let this sink in, for it is God's truth. Amen.

Let us pray:

Oh Lord, I pray that You will become our teacher. It is sad when people try to lead others without being led by You in the first place. This is when heretical teachings about You are taught. If only people would keep to the Bible, for it contains much power and great authority. It is awful to see people take certain parts of it and change it. Fewer people are receiving Your wisdom and power because of this. Many false churches come about saying that their teachings are more important than even the Bible. They say that their church leaders can contradict, speak against, or take away important verses in the Bible. How their leader's advice is more important than Your Words in scripture. This is corruption in the making, and I pray for people who are currently stuck in a religion like this that does not save. Open their eyes to what is true. May they cling to what is good and throw out what is evil. It must be hard for people who were brought up in a faith that appears to be good to leave it behind for Your name's sake. All I know, God, is that it is worth giving up things in order to be saved. I trust in You, Lord. I believe in You, God. I love You. Amen.

Chapter 12

Jesus Atoned For Our Sins In The Garden

The Book of Mormon teaches that Jesus paid the price for our sins in the garden, not simply on the cross. This is a damnable heresy, while taking away the importance of the cross. Paul taught that if anyone comes teaching another gospel, let him be accursed. He said, "I marvel that ye are so soon removed from him that called you into the grace of Christ unto another gospel: Which is not another; but there be some that trouble you, and would pervert the gospel of Christ. But though we, or an angel from heaven, preach any other gospel unto you than that which we have preached unto you, let him be accursed. As we said before, so say I now again, If any man preach any other gospel unto you than that ye have received, let him be accursed." (Galatians 1:6-9) To teach a false gospel is to bring curses upon our lives from God. So, let's now examine Mosiah, chapter 3, where the garden atonement teaching is taught.

Speaking of Jesus in Gethsemane, or the garden, the Book of Mormon reads, "and lo, he shall suffer temptations, and pain of body, hunger, thirst, and fatigue, even more than man can suffer, except it be unto death; for behold, blood cometh from every pore, so great shall be his anguish for the wickedness and the abominations of his people." (Mosiah 3:7) In this passage, we learn that Jesus suffered for our sins in the garden, and bled from every pore. This is a common teaching in Mormonism. They say it gives more insight to what we see in Luke. It is written, "And he was withdrawn from them about a stone's cast, and kneeled down, and prayed, saying, Father, if thou be willing, remove this cup from me: nevertheless not my will, but thine, be done. And there appeared an angel unto him from heaven, strengthening him. And being in an agony he prayed more earnestly: and his sweat was as it were great drops of blood falling down to the ground." (Luke 22:41-44)

Luke doesn't mention the payment for sins in the garden, as this concept is only found in the Book of Mormon. Mormons believe that Jesus began the atonement in the garden as described in the Book of Mosiah and completed it on the cross. The verses teach that Jesus's suffering is for the wickedness, and abominations of the people. He would suffer for the sins of people but not die. On the other hand, the Bible tells a different story. How in the garden, Jesus asked the Father to remove the cup of suffering, which is the cross. He was in deep thought when it came to this next event, and angels came to strengthen Him. He then began to sweat, which it came pouring down like blood does. Nothing about this act of sweating, or Jesus's anguish in the garden, is later spoken of in the Bible. However, Joseph Smith thought to add this to the narrative in the Book of Mormon. This way people would get a new understanding of what took place in the garden.

Thankfully, the Bible tells us where the atonement takes place. Paul taught that through Jesus's death, atonement was made for us. It is written, "But God commendeth his love toward us, in that, while we were yet sinners, Christ died for us. Much more then, being now justified by his blood, we shall be saved from wrath through him. For if, when we were enemies, we were reconciled to God by the death of his Son, much more, being reconciled, we shall be saved by his life. And not only so, but we also joy in God through our Lord Jesus Christ, by whom we have now received the atonement." (Romans 5:8-11) Notice that through the death of Jesus we receive the atonement. This is not acceptable in Mormonism. Instead, they put up with a false gospel that involves a garden atonement.

Mormons also love to go to Isaiah 53, which talks about Jesus's suffering. What people don't realize is it is speaking of Jesus's sacrifice on the cross. It is written, "He is despised and rejected of men; a man of sorrows, and acquainted with grief: and we hid as it were our faces from him; he was despised, and we esteemed him not. Surely he hath borne our griefs, and carried our sorrows: yet we did esteem him stricken, smitten of God, and afflicted. But he was wounded for our transgressions, he was bruised for our iniquities: the chastisement of our peace was upon him; and with his stripes we are healed." (Isaiah 53:3-5) The LDS people teach that Isaiah was prophesying of Jesus suffering in the garden. They also mention the time when Jesus was whipped, and explain that everything from what happened in the garden to the cross is part of the atonement process. What they don't realize is that atonement means blood sacrifice, and that this happened when Jesus died on the cross.

What Mormons don't realize is that Peter knew about the verses in Isaiah 53. He even clarified what the verses mean. It is written, "For even hereunto were ye called: because Christ also suffered for us, leaving us an example, that ye should follow his steps: Who did no sin, neither was guile found in his mouth: Who, when he was reviled, reviled not again; when he suffered, he threatened not; but committed himself to him that judgeth righteously: Who his own self bare our sins in his own body on the tree, that we, being dead to sins, should live unto righteousness: by whose stripes ye were healed." (1 Peter 2:21-24) The mention of stripes and being healed is spoken of again, and the place of this suffering is the tree. This is clarified in other translations as the cross. It is written, "and He Himself brought our sins in His body up on the cross, so that we might die to sin and live for righteousness; by His wounds you were healed." (1 Peter 2:24 NASB) Therefore, Jesus suffered for our sins on the cross. As Romans 5 teaches, we receive the atonement with Jesus's blood sacrifice and death.

Paul said, "but I fear, lest by any means, as the serpent beguiled Eve through his subtilty, so your minds should be corrupted from the simplicity that is in Christ. For if he that cometh preacheth another Jesus, whom we have not preached, or if ye receive another spirit, which ye have not received, or another gospel, which ye have not accepted, ye might well bear with him." (2 Corinthians 11:3,4)

Let's identify what the gospel message is. It is written, "moreover, brethren, I declare unto you the gospel which I preached unto you, which also ye have received, and wherein ye stand; By which also ye are saved, if ye keep in memory what I preached unto you, unless ye have believed in vain. For I delivered unto you first of all that which I also received, how that Christ died for our sins according to the scriptures; And that he was buried, and that he rose again the third day according to the scriptures." (1 Corinthians 15:1-4) Jesus died for our sins, was buried, and rose from the grave. This is the true gospel message, and we reject the additional garden atonement for sins. Adding to the atonement is a false gospel. There are consequences for those who reject the true gospel message in the Bible. Paul said, "in flaming fire taking vengeance on them that know not God, and that obey not the gospel of our Lord Jesus Christ: Who shall be punished with everlasting destruction from the presence of the Lord, and from the glory of his power." (2 Thessalonians 1:8,9)

Let's examine the verses in Luke one more time. It is written, "and when he was at the place, he said unto them, Pray that ye enter not into temptation. And he was withdrawn from them about a stone's cast, and kneeled down, and prayed, Saying, Father, if thou be willing, remove this cup from me: nevertheless not my will, but thine, be done. And there appeared an angel unto him from heaven, strengthening him. And being in an agony he prayed more earnestly: and his sweat was as it were great drops of blood falling down to the ground." (Luke 22:40-44)

The Mormon people have misinterpreted different verses of the Bible. This can be seen by examining the verses in Luke, chapter 22. They believe that Jesus paid the penalty for our sins while praying in the garden. This is such an abominable teaching, and it causes God's wrath to fall upon them. It is a heresy to say that Jesus paid the penalty for our sins outside the cross. The Bible is clear about this, as it reads, "knowing that Christ being raised from the dead dieth no more; death hath no more dominion over him. For in that he died, he died unto sin once: but in that he liveth, he liveth unto God." (Romans 6:9,10) The penalty for our sins was paid for at the moment Jesus died. Paul said that Jesus died unto sin once, which means the atonement happened on the cross alone. The parts in the Bible before the cross are not part of the atonement. This includes the portion in Luke, chapter

22. Jesus's sweat simply appeared like blood falling to the ground and nothing more. Adding to these verses, where it says nothing about an atonement being made in the garden, causes others to stumble.

While examining Luke, chapter 22, we see Jesus praying for comfort, and the cup representing the cross. The cup speaks of the suffering Jesus would soon go through as he would be raised up on the cross. Sweat is not blood in these passages. Even if it was, it would not be for sin. Jesus died once for sin and Satan hates every part of what happened that day. For this reason, the devil came up with a game plan. He would cause millions of people to think differently about the atonement. This was to shift people's focus from the cross and to the garden. It is the garden atonement teaching that came from this. He was thrilled to see people listen to Joseph Smith, and later so-called prophets take away from what Jesus did for us on the cross. It is the Book of Mormon that pushes this message forward. As we learned in the book of Mosiah, chapter 3, it teaches this garden atonement, where Jesus bled from every poor, of which He suffered for the sins of the people. Satan helped create this book through Joseph Smith, while teaching a false atonement in its pages. This was to lead as many people astray as he could. Millions of Mormon people are now under his deceptive grasp.

Although the Book of Mormon may appear harmless to the reader, it contains damnable heresies. As mentioned previously, Mosiah, chapter 3, contains these heretical teachings. It is written, "and lo, he shall suffer temptations, and pain of body, hunger, thirst, and fatigue, even more than man can suffer, except it be unto death; for behold, blood cometh from every pore, so great shall be his anguish for the wickedness and the abominations of his people." (Mosiah 3:7) Mormons teach that Jesus bled from every pore. This is while he was suffering in the garden. What they don't always realize is this belief has formed while reading this book and listening to their false prophets. This false belief, pertaining to the garden atonement, now appears to be true to them. It doesn't matter that atonement has always occurred with an animal's death, where Jesus is the last sacrifice for sin. He died that we might be cleansed through His blood. Therefore, I am pleading to God that the LDS people will allow You to themselves of their false beliefs. I did this in 2012 and am so happy. It was better to give up what was false for God's sake, than to stay in a place that felt comfortable. Amen.

Let us pray:

Oh Lord, I pray that the Mormon people will come to know the importance of the cross. How this is the place where You paid the penalty for our sins, and no other. It is blasphemy to add the garden to the atonement. I am deeply disturbed by the teachings of the Book of Mormon that suggests that the payment for sins began in the garden. I rebuke these false teachings. If only people would stop reading the Book of Mormon and read the Bible, things would be different. They would understand that You died for our sins on the cross, Jesus. Thank You, Lord, for taking upon yourself our sins, that we might come to You and be saved. I give You my life, my everything. Forgive me, Lord. I trust in You, God. I love You. Amen.

Chapter 13

Jesus's Blood Covers Sins Before His Birth

Without God leading a church, many things can creep in without people knowing it. False doctrines can be instituted as if they came from God. These times we live in are very dark, so we must be alert and willing to test all religious teachings to see if they are correct. In so doing, if any religion adds another book of scripture, we must test it. The Bible is the Word of God, and I challenge any other book that says it is also God's Word. Let's focus our attention on the Mormon Church. They have in their midst many other books, one of them indicates that it is "Another Testament of Jesus Christ". This is a bold claim and must be examined carefully. Instead of just throwing it out I will examine it with a fine-toothed comb. Let's do this in order to see if it is of God or not. This examination starts with the Book of Mosiah, chapter 4. In that chapter, it is recorded that before Jesus Christ's birth, people were being forgiven by the blood of Jesus. Let's examine what this really means. A few different verses will be examined in detail to see if it makes sense and is Biblical or not...

In 124 B.C, it is written, "O have mercy, and apply the atoning blood of Christ that we may receive forgiveness of our sins." (Mosiah 4:2) These people then "received a remission of their sins, and having peace of conscience, because of the exceeding faith which they had in Jesus Christ who should come." (Mosiah 4:3) If this was in the New Testament timeframe, it would make sense what the people were doing. However, seeing that Jesus's blood atonement was used prior to Jesus's birth, this indicates that Joseph Smith wrote this. It is quite astounding that Joseph Smith allowed his scribe to pencil it in. He must have had limited knowledge of the Bible. If this is not the case, then somehow, the people of the Book of Mormon thought that they could be forgiven by the blood of Jesus before His birth. This doesn't make sense since in the Old Testament times people were forgiven by animal sacrifices. See Leviticus, chapter 17, for details. Nobody was forgiven by the blood of Jesus, but were forgiven through these animal sacrifices.

Joseph Smith must not have known that people offered up animals as sacrifices for sins in the Old Testament. I mention this since in 124 B.C, people in the Book of Mormon were asking God that Jesus's atoning blood would cover their sins. See for yourself in the following verse. "And now, it came to pass that when king Benjamin had made an end of speaking the words which had been delivered unto him by the angel of the Lord, that he cast his eyes round about on the multitude, and behold they had fallen to the earth, for the fear of the Lord had come upon them. And they had viewed themselves in their own carnal state, even less than the dust of the earth. And they all cried aloud with one voice, saying: O have mercy, and apply the atoning blood of Christ that we may receive forgiveness of our sins, and our hearts may be purified; for we believe in Jesus Christ, the Son of God, who created heaven and earth, and all things; who shall come down among the children of men." (Mosiah 4:1,2) How is this possible when Jesus hadn't even been born yet? Without God coming to earth, there was no payment for sins made. Can you see an issue with these verses?

When reading the Bible, Paul helps us understand how the atonement takes place. How the atoning blood of Jesus covers people's sins, where animal sacrifices are done away with. It was in His death, that the sins of all men and women were paid for. It is written, "but God commendeth his love toward us, in that, while we were yet sinners, Christ died for us. Much more then, being now justified by his blood, we shall be saved from wrath through him. For if, when we were enemies, we were reconciled to God by the death of his Son, much more, being reconciled, we shall be saved by his life. And not only so, but we also joy in God through our Lord Jesus Christ, by whom we have now received the atonement." (Romans 5:8-11) If only people would receive Jesus into their lives, then they could be sanctified through His blood. The Lamb of God came down from heaven and died for our sins. Christ's death on the cross fulfilled the need for blood atonement done through animals. Around 124 B.C, these animal sacrifices would have been expected in the Book of Mormon. It was a mistake, adding the part about Jesus's blood atonement in that timeframe.

While living in the Old Testament times, the name "Jesus" was not known, let alone used to pray for the redemption of people's sins. So, when we spot things like this, where somehow people in the Book of Mormon were aware of the name Jesus, but the people of the Bible did not, this should cause some concern. Those who are avid Bible readers would spot this right away. As for when the blood atonement took place, it was after Jesus came to earth and died for our sins on the cross. In His death, we receive the atonement. God became flesh and dwelt among us before giving His life as a ransom for mankind. Jesus "died for our sins according to the scriptures." (1 Corinthians 15:3) His blood was shed for us on the cross. Through His atoning sacrifice, we can come to the Lord and be forgiven. There is true mercy for the sinful things we do in this life. As for the Book of Mormon people, received knew to call upon His Name for mercy until Jesus came. Do not trust the Book of Mormon as it is fictional and not of God. Beware of false teachers, prophets, churches and books. It is important to keep your eyes open so that you may not be led astray.

As Christians, we know the importance of the cross. It is essential to the gospel of Jesus and vital to understand its importance. The Bible teaches that we are saved through the blood of Jesus, that was spilled for us on the cross. This is in stark contrast with what we see in the LDS faith. They believe that the people in the Book of Mormon were forgiven by Jesus before his birth. Because this is a big problem, let's look at Mosiah, chapter 4, once again. It is written, "O have mercy, and apply the atoning blood of Christ that we may receive forgiveness of our sins, and our hearts may be purified; for we believe in Jesus Christ." (Mosiah 4:2). I see two problems here. Jesus hadn't died on the cross yet and His name was never mentioned in the Old Testament timeframe. Can you also see the conflict here? Mormons read the Book of Mormon but cannot see these issues? The fact that Joseph Smith continued to place events such as forgiveness of sins before Jesus had even been born, demonstrates how little he knew of the Bible. Christians know that forgiveness through the blood of Jesus happened on the cross, not before His birth. See 1 Corinthians 15:1-4 for details.

If you read the Bible, you will see why this is very wrong and how this could not have happened at all before Christ came to earth.

The whole purpose of Jesus coming to this world was to pay the price for our sins. Speaking of His birth, it is recorded, "she will bring forth a Son, and you shall call His name Jesus, for He will save His people from their sins." (Matthew 1:21) For so many years, people waited for a Savior. Jesus is that person, and we now have free access to Him and His mercy. The cross gives us hope for a new day. Through His mercy, we are covered by His blood. Not before Jesus came but because He did and died for us, our sins can be covered. The Bible teaches that the blood of Jesus is vital to our salvation. Our sins can be covered, because of the cross. Jesus died for us so that we can be forgiven and considered worthy. Before Christ came to earth, it was a different story as things happened much differently. People that lived before Christ, looked for the God of Israel to save them. The high priests were responsible for performing burnt offerings to atone for the sins of the people. They built altars and performed animal sacrifices. There was no forgiveness by the blood of Jesus but a sin offering, through the blood of the animal. These verses can be found in Leviticus, chapter 17.

The world underwent a profound transformation when Jesus descended and took on human flesh. This is especially true when Jesus died on the cross for the payment of our sins. We can ask for forgiveness by calling upon His Name. He is the last sacrifice for sins. He is the Lamb of God. After Jesus died on the cross, the doors were opened to be forgiven by His blood. The Book of Mormon teaching is contrary to God. If it was in line with the Bible, there would be burnt offering for their sins in Mosiah, chapter 4, but instead they thought Jesus's blood would cover them before His birth. Can you now see how this doesn't make sense, making the Book of Moron false? If you think about it clearly, these extra Biblical teachings don't make sense. It goes against the core principles of Jesus and Him dying on the cross. For this reason, I declare to the world that the Book of Mormon is a fraud. I was once a part of this church, but evidence like this is enough to have me know the book is not of God. If you are a Mormon, how do you refute these verses in Mosiah? I pray that your heart is open. Read the Bible and don't be so fast as to accept what you believe is true from books like this. Compare and contrast your beliefs with the Bible. The truth of God will set you free. Amen.

Let us pray:

Oh Lord, will you open the eyes of the blind? Will you help those who are lost to see Your truth? What is true is plain to see for those that seek You. You have unfolded to me Your mysteries and the veil has been lifted. I was blind but can now see. I once put my trust in man, but You have awakened my soul to trust in You. Thank you for leading me from darkness and into your light. For many years I thought the truth was before me. I would not accept anything but what my church taught me. Saying anything contrary to what the church said was beneath me. But Lord, You saw how closed-minded I was. I needed something to help me think clearly. In sin, You came to me. My heart was open, and You rescued me. Your mercy and forgiveness are real, for I have felt it. Because of You, I am filled with hope. You have taken my hand and led me on Your path. You have set me on a course to heaven, while helping me leave false teachings behind. It is better to live for You than to live for people that cannot save. I will continue to compare the teachings of men to the Bible. Your words are true and are a delight to my soul. I love You. I praise Your holy Name. Amen.

Chapter 14

Jesus's Name In His Church's Name

Those who are LDS believe that Christ's church needs to have His name in it. Notice in the name of their church, Jesus's name is in it. And so, they claim that they are Christ's church. LDS missionaries say that they are doing God's will because Jesus's Name is on their name tag. But anyone can slap Jesus's name on things and claim they are for God. Mormons get the belief that Jesus's name has to be in His Church's name because of the following verses in their Book of Mormon. Jesus is supposedly speaking when He said this. "And Jesus again showed himself unto them, for they were praying unto the Father in his name; and Jesus came and stood in the midst of them, and said unto them: What will ye that I shall give unto you?" (3 Nephi 27:2) "And how be it my church save it be called in my name? For if a church be called in Moses' name then it be Moses' church; or if it be called in the name of a man then it be the church of a man; but if it be called in my name then it is my church, if it so be that they are built upon my gospel." (3 Nephi 27:8) Therefore, they use this verse to prove that Jesus's will be in His church's name or else it is false and not of God.

The question is, does the Bible speak of Jesus's name being required in His church's name? Absolutely not. Read the following verses for yourself. This first church is called, "Church of God." It is written, "take heed therefore unto yourselves, and to all the flock, over the which the Holy Ghost hath made you overseers, to feed the church of God, which he hath purchased with his own blood." (Acts 20:28) The second church is called, "Church of The Living God." It is written, "but if I tarry long, that thou mayest know how thou oughtest to behave thyself in the house of God, which is the church of the living God, the pillar and ground of the truth." (1 Timothy 3:15) And the third church is called, "Church of The Firstborn." It is written, "to the general assembly and church of the firstborn, which are written in heaven, and to God the Judge of all, and to the spirits of just men made perfect." (Hebrews 12:23) The Book of Revelation references many churches in different cities, like Ephesus and more. So, if anybody says that Jesus's name must be in the church's name, what will you tell them? We can use the word of God to show people that this is not true. Therefore, what the Book of Mormon teaches about God's church is a major contradiction with the Bible. The books conflict with one another.

There is no religion that can save a person from their sins and lead them to heaven. Jesus alone has the power to save. Anyone who disagrees is a fraud and has no authority from God. He doesn't send people to tell lies, but the devil does. I often wonder how bishops, priests and pastors get the nerve to tell their congregation that only their church's baptism saves. These are wolves in sheep's clothing. This teaching is hypocrisy when compared to what God's Word teaches on this topic. If these people would read the Bible, then they would know that Christ is the head of the church. We as His true believers make up His body. It is not a building or religion that saves anyone, but through God's grace can a person be saved. People in the Church Of Jesus Christ Of Latter-Day Saints need to repent for teaching that only their church's baptism counts. The Mormon church is not grounded on Jesus, but their own self-made religion. It is not unto salvation. To tell a person that their religion is the one true church is false. A baptism in their church doesn't do anything but adds to its membership. Jesus is Lord. Only He has the power to save us from our sins.

Believers in Christ are the members of His body. Each person has a gift from God, in which the Lord uses in His church. It is written, "for as the body is one, and hath many members, and all the members of that one body, being many, are one body: so also is Christ." (1 Corinthians 12:12) Jesus "is the head of the body, the church: who is the beginning, the firstborn from the dead." (Colossians 1:18) Paul said, "for by one Spirit are we all baptized into one body, whether we be Jews or Gentiles, whether we be bond or free; and have been all made to drink into one Spirit. For the body is not one member, but many." (1 Corinthians 12:13,14) There are believers in a variety of different Bible-believing churches. Out of them are found true believers in Jesus, and are His members. Those who believe in and follow Jesus are part of His true church. Jesus is the only way to heaven, not a specific religion or denomination. Salvation comes through Christ alone and no other. Do not be deceived. Lastly, Paul said, "in the body of his flesh through death, to present you holy and unblameable and unreproveable in his sight." (Colossians 1:22) This type of faith in Jesus will save your soul from death to life eternal. Amen.

Let us pray:

Oh Lord, I pray that people of different churches will wake up to their false beliefs. These false church leaders are wolves in sheep's clothing and need to repent for leading people astray. It is very sad to see people be duped by their false teachings. But I know how convincing the spirit of the devil really is. Truly, Satan is the father of all lies. He has the power to deceive the very elect and make them doubt Your gospel message and teachings. Lord, I love Your truth. Not what I think is true, but what You have revealed to me through the Bible and through prayer. One thing I know is that not every person has all the right answers. For this reason, we must check our beliefs with Your Words, then can You lead us out of every false way and into the knowledge of the truth. Thank You for taking me out of the darkness and into Your light. I was lost in my own pride, willful sins, and unbelief until You found me. You had compassion for my soul. Truly, I did not know that You were such a merciful God until Your peace came over me, and I was forgiven. It is my prayer that more people experience Your matchless love, while in Your presence. I love You, Jesus. I give You glory. Amen.

Chapter 15

Jesus's Name Used Before His Birth

Nearly every single chapter of the Book of Mormon is a contradiction of the Bible. 2 Nephi, chapter 26, is just one of those chapters. It's funny how bad these verses are when you consider the timeframe they were written in. They claim that in the year 559 B.C., the people in this book knew the name of Jesus. These verses read, "for the Spirit of the Lord will not always strive with man. And when the Spirit ceaseth to strive with man then cometh speedy destruction, and this grieveth my soul. And as I spake concerning the convincing of the Jews, that Jesus is the very Christ, it must needs be that the Gentiles be convinced also that Jesus is the Christ, the Eternal God; And that he manifesteth himself unto all those who believe in him, by the power of the Holy Ghost; yea, unto every nation, kindred, tongue, and people, working mighty miracles, signs, and wonders, among the children of men according to their faith." (2 Nephi 26:11-13) Joseph Smith wrote the name Jesus, Jesus Christ, and Jesus the Christ, in his book in order for it to sound Biblical. Therefore, these people are more privileged to know the name of Jesus than even His people in Israel.

The Book of Mormon has many references to the name Jesus, Christ or Jesus Christ. See 2 Nephi, chapters 25,26,30,31, and 33 as just a few examples. There are many other chapters too. The point of the matter is that the Lord's Name is being used before His birth. This is the case in most of the chapters except for those starting in 3 Nephi, chapter 11. The Bible does not reveal the Name, Jesus, until his genealogy was written in Matthew, chapter 1. This is when the angel Gabriel came to Joseph and told him to name the baby, Jesus. Knowing this, it is apparent that Jesus's name was added to Joseph's book without thinking of the consequences. With the Lord's name not being mentioned until His glorious birth, this is a glaring problem. Having Jesus's name in a book makes it sound better, but doesn't make it true. It claims to be "Another Testament of Jesus Christ", but is it? Seeing how Jesus is supposedly speaking to the people, this doesn't automatically make it scripture. Visitations from Jesus are fine, but the knowledge of His name before his birth is not. Seeing that this is the case, and that many people knew His name before coming to earth, makes this book fiction. It is a clear sign that this book is false. Do not trust it.

In the Bible, you will see that there are no references to the Name, Jesus, Christ or Jesus Christ, until Matthew 1:1. It is written, "the book of the generation of Jesus Christ, the son of David, the son of Abraham. Now the birth of Jesus Christ was on this wise: When as his mother Mary was espoused to Joseph, before they came together, she was found with child of the Holy Ghost. Then Joseph her husband, being a just man, and not willing to make her a public example, was minded to put her away privily. But while he thought on these things, behold, the angel of the Lord appeared unto him in a dream, saying, Joseph, thou son of David, fear not to take unto thee Mary thy wife: for that which is conceived in her is of the Holy Ghost. And she shall bring forth a son, and thou shalt call his name Jesus: for he shall save his people from their sins." (Matthew 1:1,18-21) This is the first written account in the Bible where Jesus's name is given to mankind. Nowhere in the Old Testament is His name used like this. Only with Jesus's genealogy do we learn about His name. I conclude that the Bible can be trusted and the Book of Mormon cannot, as Jesus's name was not known before His birth.

Nobody knew or used the name Jesus, or Christ in the Old Testament. The Book of Mormon people were not more important than God's people in Israel. If anything, you see Joseph Smith's words in these deceitful writings. I'll give him credit for trying to make different verses sound Biblical. Truly, the devil uses a false prophet to make people believe in a false book. Paul warned us about giving in to false teachers. Don't believe in these lies that come from the Book of Mormon. These are fictional characters that appear to be real. It is written, "for such are false apostles, deceitful workers, transforming themselves into the apostles of Christ. And no marvel; for Satan himself is transformed into an angel of light. Therefore, it is no great thing if his ministers also be transformed as the ministers of righteousness; whose end shall be according to their works." (2 Corinthians 11:13-15) It is my invitation for every member of the LDS church to take a hard look at the Old Testament. Jesus's name was not known then, and therefore, it would not be in the Book of Mormon also. Amen.

Let us pray:

Oh Lord, thank You for showing me different issues in the Book of Mormon. Those include the blatant falsehood of people in the Book of Mormon knowing Your name before Your birth. Where people in Israel did not. If this knowledge was readily available, wouldn't your own people be aware of it? Sure, the Book sounds Biblical, but only because Your name is woven into its pages from the beginning. This doesn't make sense when we examine the same timeline in the Bible. Your name remained unknown until the angel Gabriel revealed it to Mary and Joseph. I believe that the account in Matthew is the first time Your name was spoken. Open the eyes of the LDS people, that they may see. It is a big red flag to see Your name in their book before Your birth, Jesus. Thank You for showing me how serious an issue this really is. I love You, Lord. Have Your way in my life. Amen.

Chapter 16

Jesus Was Born In Jerusalem

Mormons insist that the Book of Mormon is correct about Jerusalem being the birthplace of Jesus. They say that Bethlehem is in Jerusalem, so they justify it. However, Bethlehem is south of Jerusalem, roughly 6.2 miles away. The prophecy of Jesus's birth was specific to the town of Bethlehem in Micah, chapter 5. We will look at Matthew, chapter 2, where the priests and scribes of King Herod tell of the birthplace of Jesus, the Messiah. It is in this chapter that the three Wise Men went to Jerusalem looking for the King of the Jews, who was to be born. The star had been leading them to Jerusalem and would continue to lead them to their destination. Given word that Bethlehem was where Jesus would be born, the Wise Men went to find the promised babe. It was then that they continued their journey and found themselves where Jesus laid. They came to Him and worshiped the baby Jesus. Now, let's look at the true prophecy of Jesus's birth, along with a false prophecy...

"But behold, the Spirit hath said this much unto me, saying: Cry unto this people, saying—Repent ye, and prepare the way of the Lord, and walk in his paths, which are straight; for behold, the kingdom of heaven is at hand, and the Son of God cometh upon the face of the earth. And behold, he shall be born of Mary, at Jerusalem which is the land of our forefathers, she being a virgin, a precious and chosen vessel, who shall be overshadowed and conceive by the power of the Holy Ghost, and bring forth a son, yea, even the Son of God." (Alma 7:9,10)

"But thou, Bethlehem Ephratah, though thou be little among the thousands of Judah, yet out of thee shall he come forth unto me that is to be ruler in Israel; whose goings forth have been from of old, from everlasting." (Micah 5:2)

"Now when Jesus was born in Bethlehem of Judaea in the days of Herod the king, behold, there came wise men from the east to Jerusalem, saying, Where is he that is born King of the Jews? for we have seen his star in the east, and are come to worship him. When Herod the king had heard these things, he was troubled, and all Jerusalem with him. And when he had gathered all the chief priests and scribes of the people together, he demanded of them where Christ should be born. And they said unto him, In Bethlehem of Judaea: for thus it is written by the prophet, and thou Bethlehem, in the land of Juda, art not the least among the princes of Juda: for out of thee shall come a Governor, that shall rule my people Israel. Then Herod, when he had privily called the wise men, enquired of them diligently what time the star appeared. And he sent them to Bethlehem, and said, Go and search diligently for the young child; and when ye have found him, bring me word again, that I may come and worship him also." (Matthew 2:1-8)

If you look at a map, Jerusalem and Bethlehem are in two different places. They are not a suburb of one another, like LDS believe. To say that someone was born in Jerusalem means they were born in Jerusalem and not in Bethlehem. The same goes with people that say they are in Jerusalem. This does not mean they also went to Bethlehem. However, the Book of Mormon claims that Jesus was born in Jerusalem. This is a contradiction to what the Bible says. Let's look at this in more detail as we examine this verse in Alma, chapter 7. It reads, "but behold, the Spirit hath said this much unto me, saying: Cry unto this people, saying—Repent ye, and prepare the way of the Lord, and walk in his paths, which are straight; for behold, the kingdom of heaven is at hand, and the Son of God cometh upon the face of the earth. And behold, he shall be born of Mary, at Jerusalem which is the land of our forefathers, she being a virgin, a precious and chosen vessel, who shall be overshadowed and conceive by the power of the Holy Ghost, and bring forth a son, yea, even the Son of God." (Alma 7:9,10)

Is Bethlehem the land of our forefathers? No. Jerusalem is. Therefore, these passages in the Book of Mormon are referencing Jerusalem alone. This is in contrast to the Bible, where Jesus was born in Bethlehem. It is written, "now when Jesus was born in Bethlehem of Judaea in the days of Herod the king, behold, there came wise men from the east to Jerusalem, saying, Where is he that is born King of the Jews? for we have seen his star in the east, and are come to worship him." (Matthew 2:1,2) Herod's chief priests and scribes also quoted from Micah, chapter 5, verse 2, in reference to Jesus being born. It reads, "and thou Bethlehem, in the land of Juda, art not the least among the princes of Juda: for out of thee shall come a Governor, that shall rule my people Israel." (Matthew 2:6) Micah, a prophet of God, knew that

Jesus would be born in Bethlehem. Therefore, what we see in Alma, chapter 7, is a clear contradiction to the Bible. Jesus was supposed to be born in Jerusalem.

The Book of Mormon is wrong about the location of Jesus' birth. This is a contradiction, seeing that the Bible says that Jesus was born in Jerusalem. It is up to you how you want to respond to these accusations. You can hate me for exposing what is false or appreciate what I have done by helping people come to know the truth of God. From this message, persecution will come from the Mormon community. I will get a lot of backlash for attempting to lead people out of their church and to Christianity. My response to all Mormons is: You can come and join us at our services at Calvary Chapel. There are many wonderful Bible-believing churches out there, and Calvary Chapel is just one of them. The fact of the matter is that being part of a specific denomination or non-denominational church will not save you. Jesus saves people from all church buildings. This is difficult, however, when a false gospel is being taught. This results in an entire community that is lost as a result of it. In conclusion, Jesus was born in the town of Bethlehem two thousand years ago. He died for our sins, was buried, and rose from the grave the third day. Amen.

Let us pray:

Oh Lord, thank You for giving me clear guidance and direction when it comes to seeing what is true and what is false. For many years of my life, I thought I knew the truth about You and how to go to heaven, but it was all for naught. Everything I had ever learned about working my way to heaven was a lie. And I give You thanks for helping me know this for a fact. You have helped me understand that the Bible is the Word of God. People can slap the name Jesus on their book, church, or a name tag, but it doesn't mean it is for You in any way. Lord, the time that we are living in is very dark. Not only are there many corrupt churches like in Mormonism, that it can be hard to know what is true in this life. As Mormons are led astray by their false prophets, we have church leaders who are also leading their congregation astray by denying what the Bible says about sin. Lord, help us to know Your will and to also be willing to deny what is false and sinful in our lives for your sake. It is worth it. I love You, God. Amen.

Chapter 17

The Lake Of Fire

If there is a smoking gun for the Book of Mormon being false, it comes from 2 Nephi, chapter 9. It reads, "and assuredly, as the Lord liveth, for the Lord God hath spoken it, and it is his eternal word, which cannot pass away, that they who are righteous shall be righteous still, and they who are filthy shall be filthy still; wherefore, they who are filthy are the devil and his angels; and they shall go away into everlasting fire, prepared for them; and their torment is as a lake of fire and brimstone, whose flame ascendeth up forever and ever and has no end." (2 Nephi 9:16) This one verse is a rip-off of four different verses in the New Testament portion of the Bible. Joseph Smith took one verse out of Matthew and three additional verses from Revelation. He then combined them into one verse. Those verses from the Bible are found below...

"Then shall he say also unto them on the left hand, Depart from me, ye cursed, into everlasting fire, prepared for the devil and his angels." (Matthew 25:41)

"And the smoke of their torment ascendeth up for ever and ever: and they have no rest day nor night, who worship the beast and his image, and whosoever receiveth the mark of his name." (Revelation 14:11)

"And the devil that deceived them was cast into the lake of fire and brimstone, where the beast and the false prophet are, and shall be tormented day and night for ever and ever." (Revelation 20:10)

"He that is unjust, let him be unjust still: and he which is filthy, let him be filthy still: and he that is righteous, let him be righteous still: and he that is holy, let him be holy still." (Revelation 22:11)

Looking at the verse in 2 Nephi, chapter 9, it appears that Joseph Smith believed in the lake of fire early on in life. How the wicked would be cast into the lake of fire and be tormented day and night. Even the smoke of their torment would ascend into heaven forever and ever. Although this is Biblical and sounds good in the Book of Mormon, it is still plagiarism. This chapter in the Book of Mormon was supposedly written around 559-545 B.C. Which is long before Jesus ever came to earth. Joseph Smith thought that by including references to the New Testament in his book, he could make it appear more like the Bible. However, this con man has been apprehended in the act. Be cautious when placing your trust in Joseph Smith. He is a false prophet. Lastly, it is interesting how this book teaches an eternal lake of fire for the wicked. I say this since the Mormon church does not teach this. But why do they go against their own book's teachings?

Many verses in the Book of Mormon either contradict the Bible or their own teachings. For example, a verse in Jacob, chapter 6, talks about a real lake of fire for the wicked. How people will suffer for eternity. It reads, "and according to the power of justice, for justice cannot be denied, ye must go away into that lake of fire and brimstone, whose flames are unquenchable, and whose smoke ascendeth up forever and ever, which lake of fire and brimstone is endless torment." (Jacob 6:10) This one teaching in the Book of Mormon is often overlooked, as it is looked at metaphorically. This is simply because baptisms for the dead are important to Mormons. However, all this temple work does not help people receive a second chance after death. They refuse to accept this verse and prefer to believe that people can escape this punishment. Through doing rituals for the deceased in their temples, they believe that people will escape hell and the lake of fire. I often wonder why Mormons deny the teachings in their own Book of Mormon. This book teaches the trinity (2 Nephi 31:21; Mormon 7:7), worshipping Jesus (2 Nephi 25:29), and the lake of fire (Jacob 6:10; Mosiah 5:5; Alma 34:34,35). All this said, and the LDS people do not even subscribe to these beliefs.

The truth is, when the lake of fire is spoken of in the Bible, it is a real thing. Those who are unsaved go to hell when they die. Jesus even spoke about hell more than anyone else. He said, "wherefore if thy hand or thy foot offend thee, cut them off, and cast them from thee: it is better for thee to enter into life halt or maimed, rather than having two hands or two feet to be cast into everlasting fire. And if thine eye offend thee, pluck it out, and cast it from thee: it is better for thee to enter into life with one eye, rather than having two eyes to be cast into hell fire." (Matthew 18:8,9) How people will be cast into the lake of fire after they are judged and found guilty. It is written, "but the fearful, and unbelieving, and the abominable, and murderers, and whoremongers, and sorcerers, and idolaters, and all liars, shall have their part in the lake which burneth with fire and brimstone: which is the second death." (Revelation 21:8) If a church says you can have a second chance to go to heaven when you die, run from it as fast as you can. This teaching is from the pit of hell.

Those who are LDS hate it when we bring up hell and the lake of fire. What is so odd, however, is how their own Book of Mormon teaches about these two places in detail. One such place comes from Mosiah, chapter 5. These people are making a commitment to God, where if they fall away, they will be forever separated from Him. This is where they will suffer in a place of endless torment. It is written, "and we are willing to enter into a covenant with our God to do his will, and to be obedient to his commandments in all things that he shall command us, all the remainder of our days, that we may not bring upon ourselves a never-ending torment, as has been spoken by the angel, that we may not drink out of the cup of the wrath of God." (Mosiah 5:5) So what does this mean? According to this book, those who are saved keep God's commands. Those who do not are cast off into a lake of fire. This is where baptisms for the dead can do nothing to help them. Mormons are also incapable of keeping all their covenants with God in their temples. So, we see this book and Mormon doctrines colliding with one another.

According to the Bible, those who are unsaved will be cast into the lake of fire. They will be tormented in this place forever, as smoke ascends up into heaven. They will have no rest in this awful place. It is written, "And the third angel followed them, saying with a loud voice, If any man worship the beast and his image, and receive his mark in his forehead, or in his hand, The same shall drink of the wine of the wrath of God, which is poured out without mixture into the cup of his indignation; and he shall be tormented with fire and brimstone in the presence of the holy angels, and in the presence of the Lamb: And the smoke of their torment ascendeth up for ever and ever: and they have no rest day nor night, who worship the beast and his image, and whosoever receiveth the mark of his name. Here is the patience of the saints: here are they that keep the commandments of God, and the faith of Jesus." (Revelation 14:9-12) As believers in Jesus, we are overcomers. On the other hand, Mormons are relying on their own merits to go to heaven. They have made up a god that fits their belief system. Therefore, it will be a wake-up call when people wake up in hell.

It is interesting that the Church of Jesus Christ of Latter-Day Saints is all about their temples. Saving dead people through baptisms for the dead is what they are all about, even though it goes against the teachings in their Book of Mormon. The book speaks of no second chances, and that if we were evil in this life, our spirits are sealed to the devil in the next. It reads, "ye cannot say, when ye are brought to that awful crisis, that I will repent, that I will return to my God. Nay, ye cannot say this; for that same spirit which doth possess your bodies at the time that ye go out of this life, that same spirit will have power to possess your body in that eternal world. For behold, if ye have procrastinated the day of your repentance even until death, behold, ye have become subjected to the spirit of the devil, and he doth seal you his; therefore, the Spirit of the Lord hath withdrawn from you, and hath no place in you, and the devil hath all power over you; and this is the final state of the wicked." (Alma 34:34,35) Wow! Mormons must hate these verses if they believe in baptisms for the dead.

Christians are correct about the following verse in 1 Corinthians, chapter 15. It reads, "else what shall they do which are baptized for the dead, if the dead rise not at all? why are they then baptized for the dead?" (1 Corinthians 15:29) Paul is simply asking why certain individuals were doing baptisms for dead people. They didn't believe in the resurrection but still they did these works for the dead. This is seen in verse 12. It is written, "Now if Christ be preached that he rose from the dead, how say some among you that there is no resurrection of the dead?" (1 Corinthians 15:12) This was questioned and not an accepted teaching in the church. Baptisms for the dead was spoken against in Paul the apostles time, and so it is today also. This is a false practice! After death comes judgment. There are no second chances after death according to the Bible. John wrote, "he that overcometh shall inherit all things; and I will be his God, and he shall be my son. But the fearful, and unbelieving, and the abominable, and murderers, and whoremongers, and sorcerers, and idolaters, and all liars, shall have their part in the lake which burneth with fire and brimstone: which is the second death." (Revelation 21:7,8) Therefore, we need to consider living for Jesus in this life, for there are real consequences in the next. Amen.

Let us pray:

Oh Lord, I pray that people in all the world will come to know You as their Lord and Savior. Time is ticking, and we don't know when this life will end. We also do not know when You will return, Jesus. Many people prioritize instant gratification before You. People try everything under the sun in order for the flesh to feel a certain way. Where the right way is to have the Holy Spirit lead us. Only then can we fulfill everything our heart truly needs not desires. If people learned to listen to You and do Your will, they would be so much happier in this life. Lord, I give You thanks for giving me boldness. I am able to share the gospel with others and not feel overwhelmed, burdened, or intimidated by people. All the butterflies are over because Your Spirit is with me. I should have died many times, but You have kept me going long enough to fulfill Your will on this earth. God, I don't know when my life will end, but when it does, You will take me safely home. I love You. Amen.

Chapter 18

Melchizedek Had A Father And Mother

Melchisedec is seen in Genesis when he visits with Abram. This is when he broke bread with him and they drink wine together. Abram even gave him a tenth of all he had to Melchisedec. But who is this man? It is said that he is the king of Salem and a priest of the most high God. Was he of earthly descent, having a father and mother, or heavenly descent, having no father or mother? The Book of Mormon has an answer to this . It is written, "now this Melchizedek was a king over the land of Salem; and his people had waxed strong in iniquity and abomination; yea, they had all gone astray; they were full of all manner of wickedness; But Melchizedek having exercised mighty faith, and received the office of the high priesthood according to the holy order of God, did preach repentance unto his people. And behold, they did repent; and Melchizedek did establish peace in the land in his days; therefore he was called the prince of peace, for he was the king of Salem; and he did reign under his father." (Alma 13:17,18) So we learn that Melchisedec had a father and mother. But is this Biblically sound?

Notice how in Alma, Melchisedec reigned under his father. Pay close attention to this fact, since the Bible tells an entirely different story about this amazing man. In Hebrews, chapter 7, it states that Melchisedec is without earthly descent. He was not born of a father or a mother on earth. Therefore, he came down from heaven to the earth and visited Abraham. It is written, "for this Melchisedec, king of Salem, priest of the most high God, who met Abraham returning from the slaughter of the kings, and blessed him; To whom also Abraham gave a tenth part of all; first being by interpretation King of righteousness, and after that also King of Salem, which is, King of peace; Without father, without mother, without descent, having neither beginning of days, nor end of life; but made like unto the Son of God; abideth a priest continually." (Hebrews 7:1-3) Who has no beginning days or end of life? Jesus said, "I am Alpha and Omega, the beginning and the end, the first and the last." (Revelation 22:13) The truth is, Melchizedek is Jesus. He came down among His people in Israel many times in times past.

It was after a war, that Abram and his people rescued the people of Sodom and Lot from an ambush. During this encounter, Abram met a person named Melchisedec. However, this man was different from any other person Abram had ever met. Being the king of Salem, which translates to be the king of peace, he blessed Abram, as the Lord had done in the past also. It is written, "and Melchizedek king of Salem brought forth bread and wine: and he was the priest of the most high God. And he blessed him, and said, Blessed be Abram of the most high God, possessor of heaven and earth" (Genesis 14:18,19) This blessing is much like was said to him in Genesis 12. It reads, "and I will make of thee a great nation, and I will bless thee, and make thy name great; and thou shalt be a blessing: And I will bless them that bless thee, and curse him that curseth thee: and in thee shall all families of the earth be blessed." (Genesis 12:2,3) So we have the Lord coming to bless Abram in person after he had heard His voice in the past. No wonder Abram was excited to have Him in his company and gave unto him tithes. Wouldn't you do the same if God came to visit you? I say God, because of what we will learn next.

After Melchisedec came to Abram, Abram gave unto him a tithe of everything he had. It is written, "and blessed be the most high God, which hath delivered thine enemies into thy hand. And he gave him tithes of all." (Genesis 14:20) This same Melchisedec was no mere man as I stated earlier, but was the Lord, our God, in the flesh. The writer of Hebrews writes, "for this Melchisedec, king of Salem, priest of the most high God, who met Abraham returning from the slaughter of the kings, and blessed him; To whom also Abraham gave a tenth part of all; first being by interpretation King of righteousness, and after that also King of Salem, which is, King of peace; Without father, without mother, without descent, having neither beginning of days, nor end of life; but made like unto the Son of God; abideth a priest continually." (Hebrews 7:1-3) This Melchisedec is the King of peace, or we may say the prince of peace, which Jesus is. He is also the king of righteousness, having no earthly father or mother. Jesus had not been born of Mary yet, but simply came down to bless Abram in person. This is so amazing, indeed. This kind of thing happened many times in the past, He still wants to be with us now also. Amen.

Let us pray:

Oh Lord, help us draw near to You and escape the teachings of man. So many people give in to every wind of doctrine and call it Yours. Therefore, open their eyes to what is false. Help people understand that cults only lead to hell and destruction in the next life. Only through following You can we be safe from the temptations of the devil. He surely makes things appear good on the outside, whereas on the inside it is so dark. This is what I've seen in the Mormon church. Their missionaries go out and share what they think is good news, but when checked with the Bible, it is a false gospel. Lord, I love to witness to them. They are so young but also caught up in their pride. So often they think that they have all the right answers. This is very sad to see that they have been brainwashed and cannot even tell. They are blinded by their false prophets, and so-called modern-day revelations, that they cannot see clearly. Open their eyes, God. I trust in You. You can do all things. Lead more people out of this false religion and to You alone for salvation. I love You, Jesus. Amen.

Chapter 19

Oneness Theology

"And now Abinadi said unto them: I would that ye should understand that God himself shall come down among the children of men, and shall redeem his people. And because he dwelleth in flesh he shall be called the Son of God, and having subjected the flesh to the will of the Father, being the Father and the Son— The Father, because he was conceived by the power of God; and the Son, because of the flesh; thus becoming the Father and Son— And they are one God, yea, the very Eternal Father of heaven and of earth." (Mosiah 15:1-4)

In many parts of the Book of Mormon we learn about the trinity, but in other parts we learn about the oneness of God. The Trinity is a true doctrine found in the Bible, but oneness theology is not. So let me define "oneness". It is that Jesus is the Father, making up the same person. This is opposed to the Trinity, where the Father, Son and Holy Spirit are three different persons in one God. So for there to be a teaching in the Book of Mormon that adheres to oneness, we'd have to see verses that say that the Father and Jesus are the same person. As you read above, we learn this about Jesus. In verse 2 it says, "He dwelleth in flesh he shall be called the Son of God, and having subjected the flesh to the will of the Father, being the Father and the Son." (Mosiah 15:2) Does any Mormon agree with this doctrine? Absolutely not. But why not, given that this teaching is present in their book? In their reading of this book, what do Mormons think this verse means if they don't believe the Christian interpretation?

Joseph Smith's book teaches that Jesus is the Father. It is written, "the Father, because he was conceived by the power of God; and the Son, because of the flesh; thus becoming the Father and Son." (Mosiah 15:3) But what does the Bible say about this? That the Father, Jesus, and the Holy Spirit are three different persons. The Father leads the son in all things, and Jesus sends the Holy Spirit to guide us in all truth. It is Stephen who saw Jesus on the right hand of God, making them different persons. "Behold, I see the heavens opened, and the Son of man standing on the right hand of God." (Acts 7:56) If Jesus and the Father are separate persons, then how could they be the same God in the Trinity? It's like this. The doctrine of the Holy Trinity states that the Father, Son, and Holy Spirit are one God. They exist as three different persons, all working in perfect unity. Knowing the Father, Son, and Holy Spirit make up God, this makes one God collectively, and not three. All this makes sense as there is only one true God in the Bible, not many as Mormons have been taught to believe in.

"For unto us a child is born, unto us a son is given: and the government shall be upon his shoulder: and his name shall be called Wonderful, Counsellor, The mighty God, The everlasting Father, The Prince of Peace. Of the increase of his government and peace there shall be no end, upon the throne of David, and upon his kingdom, to order it, and to establish it with judgment and with justice from henceforth even for ever. The zeal of the Lord of hosts will perform this." (Isaiah 9:6,7)

Mormons collectively tell people that they believe in the Godhead. Where Jesus is God, the Father is God, and the Holy Spirit is God. The Father is not Jesus, nor the Holy Spirit, and vice versa, but all Gods nonetheless. This differs from the Trinity, in that we believe that each person collectively makes up God. So, three persons in one being. But why do some people in Mormonism believe that Jesus is the Father? It comes from their Book of Mormon. For example, in Mosiah 16, it reads, "teach them that redemption cometh through Christ the Lord, who is the very Eternal Father. Amen." (Mosiah 16:15) This type of teaching doesn't just exist in this chapter, but in many places of the Book of Mormon. I'll be covering each of those locations in detail. Just know that the oneness theology teaching is that Jesus is the Father. People mistakenly hold to this false belief. Without the Holy Spirit, they don't know any better. What is very sad is that when you explain how the Trinity is taught in the Bible, they reject it.

People who believe in oneness theology go to this verse to make this claim. It reads, "for unto us a child is born, unto us a son is given: and the government shall be upon his shoulder: and his name shall be called Wonderful, Counsellor, The mighty God, The everlasting Father, The Prince of Peace" (Isaiah 9:6) Notice how it says that the child is the everlasting Father. And there you have it, they say. However, Jesus helped people understand what this means and said, "believest thou not that I am in the Father, and the Father in me? the words that I speak unto you I speak not of myself: but the Father that dwelleth in me, he doeth the works." (John 14:10) Notice how Jesus explains how He is in the Father and the Father is in Him. It is because the Father's spirit dwells in the Son. This is in the same fashion the Holy Spirit dwells in us. Isaiah is talking about the Father dwelling in the Son, not that He is the Father. This makes sense as the Father, Son, and Holy Spirit are one God, not three. This is what you call perfect unity.

"For there are three that bear record in heaven, the Father, the Word, and the Holy Ghost: and these three are one. And there are three that bear witness in earth, the Spirit, and the water, and the blood: and these three agree in one." (1 John 5,7,8)

It appears that Mormons are being forced to make a decision, of whom both paths are wrong. Will they continue to believe in the Godhead doctrine and reject the Book of Mormon? Or will they choose to believe in oneness theology and reject Mormonism? The Book of Mormon teaches that Jesus is the Father, rather than separate individuals. This is just one example. It is written, "and also that ye might know of the coming of Jesus Christ, the Son of God, the Father of heaven and of earth, the Creator of all things from the beginning; and that ye might know of the signs of his coming, to the intent that ye might believe on his name." (Helaman 14:12) What is happening here? It says that Jesus is the Father of heaven and earth. This is not what the Godhead or Trinity teaches. In the Godhead, Jesus is not the Father or the Holy Spirit, but separate individuals and Gods. The Trinity teaching is that God is one being with three distinct persons: the Father, Son, and Holy Spirit. The Bible also teaches that no one can see the Father and live. The Father is Spirit, being omnipresent, and able to dwell in the Son.

The Book of Mormon doesn't teach the Godhead, but oneness theology. Jesus is the Father and not a separate God. Doesn't this contradict Mormon theology? It sure does. I discussed this with various individuals who follow the LDS faith. They admit that there are problems with these verses. They don't believe that Jesus is the Father or that there is only one God. As Christians, we see the oneness theology as not of God, along with the Mormon Godhead teaching. It is because the Bible is intentional in telling us that there is only one true God in the heavens. Jesus said that when people see Him, they see the Father. This is because His Spirit dwells in Him. It is similar to someone saying, "I see the Holy Spirit in you". Therefore, if Mormons want to keep their beliefs in the Godhead, they should reject the Book of Mormon as a whole. But if their belief is that the Book of Mormon is scripture, then they should reject their church teachings instead. However, this is all wrong. The best scenario is to reject their book and their church, for only the Trinity makes sense.

"Philip saith unto him, Lord, show us the Father, and it sufficeth us. Jesus saith unto him, Have I been so long time with you, and yet hast thou not known me, Philip? he that hath seen me hath seen the Father; and how sayest thou then, Show us the Father? Believest thou not that I am in the Father, and the Father in me? the words that I speak unto you I speak not of myself: but the Father that dwelleth in me, he doeth the works. Believe me that I am in the Father, and the Father in me: or else believe me for the very works' sake." (John 14:8-11)

Not once did Jesus say that He is the Father in the Bible. He simply said that people can see the Father when they look at Him. Many people confuse what Jesus meant when He said this. That is why we will break down John, chapter 14, in detail. First off, Jesus said that when you see me, you see the Father. How is this possible, if they are separate persons and not the same? It means that the Father dwells in Jesus, not that Jesus is the Father. Jesus explained this and said that the Father's Spirit dwells inside His body, making the Father Spirit. Jesus is always guided by the Father in everything He does. The presence of the Father serves as a remarkable explanation of how the Trinity operates. We have the Father's Spirit dwelling in the Son, and the Holy Spirit dwelling in humans. They all work together in perfect unity as one God. This one God is made up of the Father, Jesus, and the Holy Spirit, although they are not the same person. The Book of Mormon tells a different story, which changes the Bible's narrative.

Instead of the Father and Son being different persons, they are the same person. This theology is referred to as oneness. Here is just one example of this teaching. It is written, "behold, I am he who was prepared from the foundation of the world to redeem my people. Behold, I am Jesus Christ. I am the Father and the Son. In me shall all mankind have life, and that eternally, even they who shall believe on my name; and they shall become my sons and my daughters." (Ether 3:14) So there you have it. No longer is the Father a different person than Jesus, His Son. This is a false teaching called Modalism. Where the Father is manifest in the Son. Although Christians know this teaching to be false, Mormons don't care that the teaching exists in their Book of Mormon. They say that modern day revelations from their false prophets trump what their book or Bible says. Therefore, they believe in the Godhead doctrine. The Father, Jesus, and the Holy Spirit make up three different Gods, being one in purpose. This is heresy. One day the LDS people will learn that there is only one true God in the heavens on judgment day.

"And Jared lived an hundred sixty and two years, and he begat Enoch: And Jared lived after he begat Enoch eight hundred years, and begat sons and daughters: And all the days of Jared were nine hundred sixty and two years: and he died. And Enoch lived sixty and five years, and begat Methuselah: And Enoch walked with God after he begat

Methuselah three hundred years, and begat sons and daughters: And all the days of Enoch were three hundred sixty and five years: And Enoch walked with God: and he was not; for God took him." (Genesis 5:18-23)

In Genesis, chapter 5, we learn about Jared. He lived around 3544-2582 B.C. I am mentioning Jared's name since you see a brother of Jared in the Book of Mormon. The alleged sibling of Jared is believed to have lived approximately in 2200 B.C. The timelines of the brother of Jared and Jared are close but still three hundred years apart. As for the Biblical text, there is no mention of another Jared during that timeframe. The Book of Mormon tries to identify this fictional character as "Mahonri Moriancumer". He supposedly came from the time when God confounded the languages during the tower of Babel. The story of that event is in Genesis 11 and dates around 2300 B.C. However, there is no evidence for this other Jared or his brother. We only hear about Enoch's grandfather, who is called Jared. He didn't make it on the boat and died beforehand. Speaking of the flood, Peter wrote, "which sometime were disobedient, when once the longsuffering of God waited in the days of Noah, while the ark was a preparing, wherein few, that is, eight souls were saved by water." (1 Peter 3:20)

So, who went into the ark? It was Noah, and his wife, Shem, Ham, Japheth, and their wives, making a total of eight people. We learn this because "Noah begat three sons, Shem, Ham, and Japheth." (Genesis 6:10) Also, when speaking of the ark, it says the following. "And Noah went in, and his sons, and his wife, and his sons' wives with him, into the ark, because of the waters of the flood." (Genesis 7:7) Therefore, only Noah's family and their wives survived the flood. As for the brother of Jared, Mormons swear that he is real. In the Book of

Mormon, it reads the following about him. "And in that day that they shall exercise faith in me, saith the Lord, even as the brother of Jared did, that they may become sanctified in me, then will I manifest unto them the things which the brother of Jared saw, even to the unfolding unto them all my revelations, saith Jesus Christ, the Son of God, the Father of the heavens and of the earth, and all things that in them are." (Ether 4:7) Based on what this person saw and heard, it suggests that both he and the forementioned Jesus are not real, but fictional characters. This is because of the oneness theology that he was taught. Where Jesus is the Father.

In the Book of Mormon, the story goes that a person named the "brother of Jared" saw Jesus before His birth. He even learned that Jesus is the Father. This is what we call oneness theology or modalism, which some people subscribe to. This line of thinking is inspired by John, chapter 14. This weird belief comes from the following verses. It is written, "believest thou not that I am in the Father, and the Father in me? the words that I speak unto you I speak not of myself: but the Father that dwelleth in me, he doeth the works. Believe me that I am in the Father, and the Father in me: or else believe me for the very works' sake. Verily, verily, I say unto you, He that believeth on me, the works that I do shall he do also; and greater works than these shall he do; because I go unto my Father." (John 14:10-12) First off, Jesus said that the Father's Spirit is in Him, not that he is the Father. He even stated that He is going to the Father, making them two persons, not one. Therefore, oneness theology is false, and so is the Mormon Godhead doctrine. The truth is, the Father, Son, and Holy Spirit are three persons in one God. This is the Trinity.

"If ye had known me, ye should have known my Father also: and from henceforth ye know him, and have seen him. Philip saith unto him,

Lord, show us the Father, and it sufficeth us. Jesus saith unto him, Have I been so long time with you, and yet hast thou not known me, Philip? he that hath seen me hath seen the Father; and how sayest thou then, Show us the Father? Believest thou not that I am in the Father, and the Father in me? the words that I speak unto you I speak not of myself: but the Father that dwelleth in me, he doeth the works. Believe me that I am in the Father, and the Father in me: or else believe me for the very works' sake. Verily, verily, I say unto you, He that believeth on me, the works that I do shall he do also; and greater works than these shall he do; because I go unto my Father." (John 14:7-12)

Has Jesus ever said that He is the Father? The answer is No. But did Jesus say that people would see the Father when they see Him? Yes, He did. There are big differences between the two. People who subscribe to the notion that Jesus is the Father are part of the oneness theology camp. The Father and Son just have different modes, which we call Modalism. See below for an example of this in the Book of Mormon, which is very disturbing. It is written, "And whatsoever thing persuadeth men to do good is of me; for good cometh of none save it be of me. I am the same that leadeth men to all good; he that will not believe my words will not believe me—that I am; and he that will not believe me will not believe the Father who sent me. For behold, I am the Father, I am the light, and the life, and the truth of the world." (Ether 4:12) This is just one example of many that I've found in the Book of Mormon, which teaches that Jesus is our Father in heaven. This is false, and so is the teaching of three different Gods in the Godhead. The true doctrine is that the Father, Jesus, and the Holy Spirit are one God. This is the Holy Trinity.

Our Father in heaven does exist, but so does His Son, Jesus. Joseph Smith must not have known this when He wrote this into His book.

The funny thing is, Mormons don't see an issue with this teaching. You can bring up the verse in Ether, chapter 4, and other places in the Book of Mormon, and they just write it off. Instead of seeing it as a contradiction to the Godhead, they won't teach on it, but at the same time they don't condemn the verses. They stick with the Godhead teaching, which says that the Father, Jesus, and the Holy Spirit are each God. So, three Gods in total. They do not believe that Jesus is the Father and admittedly teach against this. Asking a Mormon missionary if they believed that Jesus is the Father, they would say "No". And if I said that I know people who believe this way, they would say they are wrong. However, if I show them verses in their Book of Mormon that teach this, they will justify them. At the same time, they would say that I was taking different verses out of context. This is what always happens when we bring up issues in the Book of Mormon. If only they would listen. Amen.

Let us pray:

God, I am grateful to understand the Trinity. It helps me understand how false the oneness theology really is, along with the Godhead doctrine taught in Mormonism. I give You praise! The Father, Son, and Holy Spirit, three in one. I praise the Father, I praise the Son, I praise the Holy Spirit. God, Your presence brings me immense joy and fills my heart with love. Thank you, God, for being with me. I am unable to be led into all truth without You. I ask that You come and teach many people in the Mormon church also. Lead them out of bondage and into Your loving arms of freedom. May they unlearn their false beliefs and learn Your truths instead. I am talking about those who are humble. Assist me in spreading the good news of the kingdom to others. I love You, Jesus. Amen.

Chapter 20

Only One God

The Book of Mormon teaches that there is only one true God in the heavens. How can this be when their church teaches that there are multiple Gods? See for yourself the contradiction in this book and their own doctrines. Certainly, they must hate these verses in Alma, chapter 11. It is written, "and Zeezrom said unto him: Thou sayest there is a true and living God? And Amulek said: Yea, there is a true and living God. Now Zeezrom said: Is there more than one God? And he answered, No. Now Zeezrom said unto him again: How knowest thou these things? And he said: An angel hath made them known unto me." (Alma 11:26-31) Therefore, there is only one true God. This collides with what Joseph Smith taught. "You have got to learn how to be Gods yourselves; to be kings and priests to God, the same as all Gods have done; by going from a small degree to another, from grace to grace, from exaltation to exaltation, until you are able to sit in glory as doth those who sit enthroned in everlasting power." (Discourse, 7 April 1844, as Reported by Times and Seasons) Did the author of the Book of Mormon just declare that we got to learn to be Gods as other Gods have done before us? Not at all, but it's author did. This is complete heresy and a contradiction to his own book, which is crazy.

Joseph Smith didn't just write the Book of Mormon, he had help from friends and family. They all believed in the one true God, and Him alone. However, this changed shortly after starting the Mormon church. The truth is, there is only one true God, and the Bible teaches this. As Christians, we teach from the Bible, whereas Mormons teach from other books more often. God's Word says, "ye are my witnesses, saith the Lord, and my servant whom I have chosen: that ye may know and believe me, and understand that I am he: before me there was no God formed, neither shall there be after me." (Isaiah 43:10) "Thou believest that there is one God; thou doest well: the devils also believe, and tremble." (James 2:19) Therefore, if Mormons ever tell you that we can be exalted to Godhood, then they don't understand the Bible. Explain to them that the Bible tells a different story. For example, in Isaiah, chapter 43, and James, chapter 2, there is only one true God. This is important to know when talking to cult members. They people are lost but cannot see this. Only when we step out in faith and share the truth of God with them, things change. This takes courage, but with God on our side, there is boldness. He gives us words to speak.

Book Of Mormon Teachings On God:
Only one true God.

"And Zeezrom said unto him: Thou sayest there is a true and living God? And Amulek said: Yea, there is a true and living God. Now Zeezrom said: Is there more than one God? And he answered, No. Now Zeezrom said unto him again: How knowest thou these things?

And he said: An angel hath made them known unto me." (Alma 11:26-31)

One God in multiple persons, the Trinity.

"And now, behold, my beloved brethren, this is the way; and there is none other way nor name given under heaven whereby man can be saved in the kingdom of God. And now, behold, this is the doctrine of Christ, and the only and true doctrine of the Father, and of the Son, and of the Holy Ghost, which is one God, without end. Amen." (2 Nephi 31:21)

"Now, this restoration shall come to all, both old and young, both bond and free, both male and female, both the wicked and the righteous; and even there shall not so much as a hair of their heads be lost; but every thing shall be restored to its perfect frame, as it is now, or in the body, and shall be brought and be arraigned before the bar of Christ the Son, and God the Father, and the Holy Spirit, which is one Eternal God, to be judged according to their works, whether they be good or whether they be evil." (Alma 11:44)

"And he hath brought to pass the redemption of the world, whereby he that is found guiltless before him at the judgment day hath it given unto him to dwell in the presence of God in his kingdom, to sing ceaseless praises with the choirs above, unto the Father, and unto the Son, and unto the Holy Ghost, which are one God, in a state of happiness which hath no end." (Mormon 7:7)

Mormon Church "False Teachings" On God:
Many gods in the heavens.

"You have got to learn how to be Gods yourselves; to be kings and priests to God, the same as all Gods have done; by going from a small degree to another, from grace to grace, from exaltation to exaltation, until you are able to sit in glory as doth those who sit enthroned in everlasting power." (Discourse, 7 April 1844, as Reported by Times and Seasons)

"In the beginning, the head of the Gods called a council of the Gods; and they came together and concocted a plan to create the world and people it," (Journal of Discourses, vol. 6, p. 5)

"And again, verily I say unto you, if a man marry a wife, and make a covenant with her for time and for all eternity, if that covenant is not by me or by my word, which is my law, and is not sealed by the Holy Spirit of promise, through him whom I have anointed and appointed unto this power, then it is not valid neither of force when they are out of the world, because they are not joined by me, saith the Lord, neither by my word; when they are out of the world it cannot be received there, because the angels and the gods are appointed there, by whom they cannot pass; they cannot, therefore, inherit my glory; for my house is a house of order, saith the Lord God." (Doctrine And Covenants 132:18)

Exaltation to Godhood.

"And again, verily I say unto you, if a man marry a wife by my word, which is my law, and by the new and everlasting covenant, and it is sealed unto them by the Holy Spirit of promise, by him who is anointed, unto whom I have appointed this power and the keys of this priesthood; and it shall be said unto them—Ye shall come forth in the first resurrection; and if it be after the first resurrection, in the next resurrection; and shall inherit thrones, kingdoms, principalities, and powers, dominions, all heights and depths—then shall it be written in the Lamb's Book of Life, that he shall commit no murder whereby to shed innocent blood, and if ye abide in my covenant, and commit no murder whereby to shed innocent blood, it shall be done unto them in all things whatsoever my servant hath put upon them, in time, and through all eternity; and shall be of full force when they are out of the world; and they shall pass by the angels, and the gods, which are set there, to their exaltation and glory in all things, as hath been sealed upon their heads, which glory shall be a fulness and a continuation of the seeds forever and ever. Then shall they be gods, because they have no end; therefore shall they be from everlasting to everlasting, because they continue; then shall they be above all, because all things are subject unto them. Then shall they be gods, because they have all power, and the angels are subject unto them." (Doctrine and Covenants 132:19,20)

"Abraham received concubines, and they bore him children; and it was accounted unto him for righteousness, because they were given unto him, and he abode in my law; as Isaac also and Jacob did none other things than that which they were commanded; and because they did none other things than that which they were commanded, they have entered into their exaltation, according to the promises, and sit upon thrones, and are not angels but are gods." (Doctrine and Covenants 132:37)

Bible Teachings On God:
One God in multiple persons, the Trinity.

"And God said, Let us make man in our image, after our likeness: and let them have dominion over the fish of the sea, and over the fowl of the air, and over the cattle, and over all the earth, and over every creeping thing that creepeth upon the earth." (Genesis 1:26)

"In the beginning was the Word, and the Word was with God, and the Word was God. The same was in the beginning with God." (John 1;1,2)

"For there are three that bear record in heaven, the Father, the Word, and the Holy Ghost: and these three are one. And there are three that bear witness in earth, the Spirit, and the water, and the blood: and these three agree in one." (1 John 5:7,8)

There is only one true God.

"Unto thee it was shewed, that thou mightest know that the Lord he is God; there is none else beside him. Know therefore this day, and consider it in thine heart, that the Lord he is God in heaven above, and upon the earth beneath: there is none else." (Deuteronomy 4:35,39)

"Wherefore thou art great, O Lord God: for there is none like thee, neither is there any God beside thee, according to all that we have heard with our ears. And what one nation in the earth is like thy people, even like Israel, whom God went to redeem for a people to himself, and to make him a name, and to do for you great things and terrible, for thy land, before thy people, which thou redeemedst to thee from Egypt, from the nations and their gods? For thou hast confirmed to thyself thy people Israel to be a people unto thee for ever: and thou, Lord, art become their God." (2 Samuel 7:22-24)

"And let these my words, wherewith I have made supplication before the Lord, be nigh unto the Lord our God day and night, that he maintain the cause of his servant, and the cause of his people Israel at all times, as the matter shall require: That all the people of the earth may know that the Lord is God, and that there is none else. Let your heart therefore be perfect with the Lord our God, to walk in his statutes, and to keep his commandments, as at this day." (1 Kings 8:59-61)

"And Hezekiah prayed before the Lord, and said, O Lord God of Israel, which dwellest between the cherubims, thou art the God, even thou alone, of all the kingdoms of the earth; thou hast made heaven and earth. Lord, bow down thine ear, and hear: open, Lord, thine eyes, and see: and hear the words of Sennacherib, which hath sent him to reproach the living God." (2 Kings 19:15,16)

"O Lord, for thy servant's sake, and according to thine own heart, hast thou done all this greatness, in making known all these great things. O Lord, there is none like thee, neither is there any God beside thee, according to all that we have heard with our ears. And what one nation in the earth is like thy people Israel, whom God went to redeem to be his own people, to make thee a name of greatness and terribleness, by driving out nations from before thy people whom thou hast redeemed out of Egypt? For thy people Israel didst thou make thine own people for ever; and thou, Lord, becamest their God." (1 Chronicles 17:19-22)

"O Lord of hosts, God of Israel, that dwellest between the cherubims, thou art the God, even thou alone, of all the kingdoms of the earth: thou hast made heaven and earth. Incline thine ear, O Lord, and hear; open thine eyes, O Lord, and see: and hear all the words of Sennacherib, which hath sent to reproach the living God.Of a truth, Lord, the kings of Assyria have laid waste all the nations, and their countries, and have cast their gods into the fire: for they were no gods, but the work of men's hands, wood and stone: therefore they have destroyed them. Now therefore, O Lord our God, save us from his hand, that all the kingdoms of the earth may know that thou art the Lord, even thou only." (Isaiah 37:16-20)

"Ye are my witnesses, saith the Lord, and my servant whom I have chosen: that ye may know and believe me, and understand that I am he: before me there was no God formed, neither shall there be after me. I, even I, am the Lord; and beside me there is no saviour. I have declared, and have saved, and I have shewed, when there was no strange god among you: therefore ye are my witnesses, saith the Lord, that I am God." (Isaiah 43:10-12)

"Thus saith the Lord the King of Israel, and his redeemer the Lord of hosts; I am the first, and I am the last; and beside me there is no God. And who, as I, shall call, and shall declare it, and set it in order for me, since I appointed the ancient people? and the things that are coming, and shall come, let them shew unto them. Fear ye not, neither be afraid: have not I told thee from that time, and have declared it? ye are even my witnesses. Is there a God beside me? yea, there is no God; I know not any." (Isaiah 44:6-8)

"I am the Lord, and there is none else, there is no God beside me: I girded thee, though thou hast not known me: That they may know from the rising of the sun, and from the west, that there is none beside me. I am the Lord, and there is none else." (Isaiah 45:5,6)

"Assemble yourselves and come; draw near together, ye that are escaped of the nations: they have no knowledge that set up the wood of their graven image, and pray unto a god that cannot save. Tell ye, and bring them near; yea, let them take counsel together: who hath declared this from ancient time? who hath told it from that time? have not I the Lord? and there is no God else beside me; a just God and a Saviour; there is none beside me. Look unto me, and be ye saved, all the ends of the earth: for I am God, and there is none else." (Isaiah 45:20-22)

"And ye shall eat in plenty, and be satisfied, and praise the name of the Lord your God, that hath dealt wondrously with you: and my people shall never be ashamed. And ye shall know that I am in the midst of Israel, and that I am the Lord your God, and none else: and my people shall never be ashamed." (Joel 2:26,27)

"Thou believest that there is one God; thou doest well: the devils also believe, and tremble." (James 2:19)

If anyone says there are other true Gods out there, or that they can become one, they do not understand the Bible. These teachings are false and are not found in the Word of God. These ideas are man-made and are blasphemy to God's words. Do we strive to know God's words and live by them? Or do we live by man-made ideas that lead to death and separation from God? Tear down all false teachings in your lives and come to know the one true God that saves. Test your faith with what the Bible says and you will know the truth of God. Those that are in the faith have God in their lives. All other gods, and ideas of gods, are cast down. The God of Israel is lifted up instead in worship. They live for Him and in His holiness, they are made righteous. Amen.

Let us pray:

Oh Lord, help me and others in the faith to be an even better witness to the Mormons. Not only do I live in a state where Mormonism is prevalent, but LDS missionaries message me often. I once thought that this was a wonderful thing, although it can be hard to get the truth across. There are many opportunities to share the gospel with them, although it is difficult. God, I did not realize how blind these people really are to the truth. What they do is share their false teachings with us, but when we tell them what the Bible says, they are often done. These individuals close up inside, and the conversation goes south. Therefore, may we have more fruitful opportunities with these cult members. If people I converse with will not hear Your truth, then I will move on to talk to other Mormons who are searching for truth. I am asking that You put people on my path who are seeking the truth. Those who want to learn. I love to speak Your truth to different crowds, but especially love to do one-on-one conversations with people. Wherever You will lead me, I will go. Open my mouth and I will speak. I am Your willing servant. Lead me this day and forever. I will do what You say. I love You, Lord. I give You praise and all the glory. You deserve it. Amen.

Chapter 21

Only One True Church

"And Jesus answered and said unto him, Blessed art thou, Simon Barjona: for flesh and blood hath not revealed it unto thee, but my Father which is in heaven. And I say also unto thee, That thou art Peter, and upon this rock I will build my church; and the gates of hell shall not prevail against it." (Matthew 16:17,18)

Jesus told His disciples that the gates of hell would not prevail against His church. This means that an apostasy is ruled out completely. People have gone astray, but His church has continued to stay strong over the centuries. As Jesus is the church, and we are His members, it would never fail. People have stopped believing, but His true believers have continued to believe in Him throughout the centuries and unto now. However, Joseph Smith claimed that Jesus told him that His church fell away into apostasy. How the churches are an abomination in His sight. It is written, "I was answered that I must join none of them, for they were all wrong; and the Personage who addressed me said that all their creeds were an abomination in his sight; that those professors were all corrupt; that: they draw near to me with their lips, but their hearts are far from me, they teach for doctrines the commandments of men, having a form of godliness, but they deny the power thereof." (Joseph Smith History 1:19)

This is not God speaking but the devil. Satan has always wanted to tear down the church that Jesus established. This has not worked out until the formation of cults over the centuries like in Mormonism. Those who are LDS believe that Christianity is false, while only their church is true. Saying such things is demonic. As for me and other Christians, we believe what Jesus said and not Joseph Smith. How Christ's church did not fall away. Paul said it this way. "For as the body is one, and hath many members, and all the members of that one body, being many, are one body: so also is Christ. For by one Spirit are we all baptized into one body, whether we be Jews or Gentiles, whether we be bond or free; and have been all made to drink into one Spirit. For the body is not one member, but many." (1 Corinthians 12:12-14) As these verses imply, the members of Christ's church exist in many different churches and denominations. We as believers are in all the world. Jesus knows who His true believers are and sorts us out.

The members of Christ's church have kept the faith and still exist today. Mormons disagree and say that only their church is true, while other churches are of the devil. It is written, "and it came to pass that he said unto me: Look, and behold that great and abominable church, which is the mother of abominations, whose founder is the devil. And he said unto me: Behold there are save two churches only; the one is the church of the Lamb of God, and the bother is the church of the devil; wherefore, whoso belongeth not to the church of the Lamb of God belongeth to that great church, which is the mother of abominations;

and she is the whore of all the earth." (1 Nephi 14:9) Don't believe the lies in the Mormon Church. There are corrupt churches out there, like the Mormon church, but Jesus's church has continued strong over the centuries. The reason why this verse exists is to keep people from joining other churches. This is mind control at its finest. The truth is, Jesus is the only way to salvation, and not religion. Amen.

Let us pray:

Oh Lord, it is sad to see a church that would cause people to doubt You and the church You established. It is terrible to see Mormons downplaying the teachings in Christianity. I am talking about the Trinity, heaven and hell, the importance of the cross, and so many other teachings. How can they feel good about their beliefs when the Book of Mormon teaches the opposite? Only the devil would want them to think only their church is true. So he added this to that book also. This evidence strongly suggests that the Book of Mormon originates from Satan. You have taught me this, Lord. Thank You, Jesus. The devil has been trying to take down Your church since it was founded, and He is now winning the souls of every Mormon. Lord, there false prophets are showing them the way instead of You and Your Word, the Bible. If people would put aside their church books and simply read the Bible and pray, their false beliefs would be removed. You can do things, Lord, as to lead people from darkness and into Your light. I trust in You, Jesus. I love You. Amen.

Chapter 22

Polygamy Is An Abomination

Mormons are known for polygamy in times past. For this reason, let's see what their different books have to say about their actions. First off, Let's compare Jacob, chapter 2, from the Book of Mormon, with Doctrine and Covenants (D&C), chapter 132. God says in Jacob that David's life of polygamy is sinful and an abomination in His sight. Whereas in D&C, David's life of polygamy is not a sin, and God was ok with it. Starting with Jacob, it is written, "and now I make an end of speaking unto you concerning this pride. And were it not that I must speak unto you concerning a grosser crime, my heart would rejoice exceedingly because of you. But the word of God burdens me because of your grosser crimes. For behold, thus saith the Lord: This people begin to wax in iniquity; they understand not the scriptures, for they seek to excuse themselves in committing whoredoms, because of the things which were written concerning David, and Solomon his son. Behold, David and Solomon truly had many wives and concubines, which thing was abominable before me, saith the Lord." (Jacob

2:22-24) This sure sounds like polygamy is wrong, but get ready for what D&C says next.

Below are the verses from D&C. It is written, "David also received many wives and concubines, and also Solomon and Moses my servants, as also many others of my servants, from the beginning of creation until this time; and in nothing did they sin save in those things which they received not of me. David's wives and concubines were given unto him of me, by the hand of Nathan, my servant, and others of the prophets who had the keys of this power; and in none of these things did he sin against me save in the case of Uriah and his wife; and, therefore he hath fallen from his exaltation, and received his portion; and he shall not inherit them out of the world, for I gave them unto another, saith the Lord." (Doctrine And Covenants 132:38,39) This sounds contrary to Jacob, doesn't it? As for the real God of the Bible, He has a view on polygamy. It is written, "neither shall he multiply wives to himself, that his heart turn not away: neither shall he greatly multiply to himself silver and gold." (Deuteronomy 17:17) Therefore, polygamy is not of God, although the gods in Mormonism are confused on this matter.

Mormons justify the early church's acts of polygamy by looking at people in the Bible and their number of wives. 2 Samuel, chapter 12, is just one example of their misinterpretations. In talking to them, they say, "God gave David his polygamist wives, so polygamy is justified in His sight." And without the Holy Spirit, we may agree with them. Therefore, we will read the verses together and discuss them in detail. It is written, "and Nathan said to David, Thou art the man. Thus saith the Lord God of Israel, I anointed thee king over Israel, and I delivered thee out of the hand of Saul; And I gave thee thy master's house, and thy master's wives into thy bosom, and gave thee the house of Israel and of Judah; and if that had been too little, I would moreover have given unto thee such and such things." (2 Samuel 12:7,8) After reading this, Mormons mention the fact that God gave David his master's wives. This is because their church is founded on polygamy that they say this. If they get this wrong, then their whole church is false. So, there is a need to clarify these verses by way and power of the Holy Spirit.

David's first wife is called Michal. She is King Saul's daughter. However, this woman was ripped apart from him because of her father's desire to kill him. Therefore, this marriage ended prematurely without their consent. Abigail came next, but he was not in a polygamist relationship with her. This happened when his lust had given him over to other women. This is when he found Ahinoam and got married. So, David had two wives from different marriages before he started getting into trouble with more wives. "Thy master's wives" is could be referring to Michal and Abigail, or David lusting after other women. It doesn't mean that God was in favor of David having more wives. Why do Mormons then say that God gave David multiple wives? Even their Book of Mormon says the opposite. "Behold, David and Solomon truly had many wives and concubines, which thing was abominable before me, saith the Lord." (Jacob 2:25) The god of Mormonism doesn't seem to agree that these multiple wives are from Him. How very interesting, and all so confusing at the same time, if you are a part of the Mormon church. Which book is right? You have to wonder if it is the Bible, Book of Mormon, or D&C.

There is evidence that Joseph Smith instituted polygamy in Mormonism, as he was a polygamist and had many wives. A message from the official LDS website confirms this. It is called, "Plural Marriage In Kirtland And Nauvoo". It is written, "Joseph told associates that an angel appeared to him three times between 1834 and 1842 and commanded him to proceed with plural marriage when he hesitated to move forward. During the third and final appearance, the angel came with a drawn sword, threatening Joseph with destruction unless he went forward and obeyed the commandment fully...Evidence indicates that Joseph Smith participated in both types of sealings. The exact number of women to whom he was sealed in his lifetime is unknown because the evidence is fragmentary...Most of those sealed to Joseph Smith were between 20 and 40 years of age at the time of their sealing to him. The oldest, Fanny Young, was 56 years old. The youngest was Helen Mar Kimball, daughter of Joseph's close friends Heber C. and Vilate Murray Kimball, who was sealed to Joseph several months before her 15th birthday." (Plural Marriage In Kirtland And Nauvoo)

It is wonderful to see the evidence of Joseph Smith's crime made readily available on the internet. His encounter with an angel of light was from Satan, and he fell for it. Even his life of polygamy goes against his own Book of Mormon. Polygamy is outlawed in that book and even called an abomination. It is written, "behold, David and Solomon truly had many wives and concubines, which thing was abominable before me, saith the Lord. Wherefore, thus saith the Lord, I have led this people forth out of the land of Jerusalem, by the power of mine arm, that I might raise up unto me a righteous branch from the fruit of the loins of Joseph. Wherefore, I the Lord God will not suffer that this people shall do like unto them of old." (Jacob 2:24-26) "Wherefore, my brethren, hear me, and hearken to the word of the Lord: For there shall not any man among you have save it be one wife; and concubines he shall have none; For I, the Lord God, delight in the chastity of women. And whoredoms are an abomination before me; thus saith the Lord of Hosts." (Jacob 2:27,28) Speaking of the overseer in God's church, they are to only have one wife. it is written, "a bishop then must be blameless, the husband of one wife, vigilant, sober, of good behaviour, given to hospitality, apt to teach." (1 Timothy 3:2) The God of the Bible is not for polygamy. Therefore, Joseph practiced it while being led by an evil spirit. Amen.

Let us pray:

Oh Lord, may every Mormon who is in doubt of their current beliefs come to know what is true from You, and You alone. Give them over to wisdom through the Bible, prayers, and true Christians. Lead them away from the doctrines of men. I love these people. Many of my family members are in it, so sharing the truth with them is the least I can do. God, it would be so amazing to see them in heaven. I truly care for them and I don't wish for people to be punished after they die. Knowing the truth of the Mormon church and that I may not see people I love in heaven is very saddening. There is much grief and sadness for the people I love. This breaks my heart. Please make a way for me to reach my siblings, parents, aunts, and others for Your cause. I feel an urgency to do this. You've helped me know that we cannot cheat death. May they receive You, Jesus, and be saved before this life is over. I've been to many funerals without any firm knowledge that these people are now in paradise. I want this to be, Lord, but know that You are just, and people go where they need to. It is my prayer that people will see You in me. I love You, Jesus. There is salvation only through You and not a church. You are enough, Lord. Amen.

Chapter 23

Priests Called To Preach The Gospel

The order from God to the priests in the tabernacle was not to be taken lightly. This was pertaining to the animal sacrifices that would be performed on the altar. The priests who did this as God directed, He would sanctify them and His tabernacle. It is written, "this shall be a continual burnt offering throughout your generations at the door of the tabernacle of the congregation before the Lord: where I will meet you, to speak there unto thee. And there I will meet with the children of Israel, and the tabernacle shall be sanctified by my glory. And I will sanctify the tabernacle of the congregation, and the altar: I will sanctify also both Aaron and his sons, to minister to me in the priest's office." (Exodus 29:42-44) The Book of Leviticus also teaches that the Israelite priests performed these sacrificial offerings at the door of the tabernacle. They did this with honor and respect to the God of the heavens. It was not a burden for them, but a joy to do His will on earth as it is in heaven.

God would be with His people as long as they continue to do His will. This was pertaining to what would take place at the door of the tabernacle. This is where offerings were made to God. These sacrifices fulfilled God's will for His people in the old covenant times. While doing these acts of faith, their sins and the sins of the people were atoned for. It is written, "and I will dwell among the children of Israel, and will be their God. And they shall know that I am the Lord their God, that brought them forth out of the land of Egypt, that I may dwell among them: I am the Lord their God." (Exodus 29:45,46) All these sacrifices ended when Jesus died for our sins on the cross. Those who accept His atoning sacrifice are forgiven and washed clean through His blood. Animal sacrifices had to happen until the Lamb of God, who is Jesus, died for us. He came into the world to take away our sins, and sanctify us once and for all. All Jesus requires is for us to come unto Him and His blood will cover us. Amen.

The Book of Mormon has priests in the same timeframe as the Bible. However, they are used differently as they were part of a church instead of God's tabernacle. For example, in Mosiah, chapter 18, priests were not called to administer in tabernacles but to go out to preach the gospel. People were also baptized before John the Baptist was born. This was during the times of the laws of Moses. They even formed Christ's Church before Jesus's birth. This is not biblical and wrong. These issues can be found while examining the chapter in Mosiah. it is written, "and after this manner he did baptize every one that went forth to the place of Mormon; and they were in number about two hundred and four souls; yea, and they were baptized in the waters of Mormon, and were filled with the grace of God. And they were called the church of God, or the church of Christ, from that time forward. And it came to pass that whosoever was baptized by the power and authority of God was added to his church. And it came to pass that Alma, having authority from God, ordained priests; even one priest to every fifty of their number did he ordain to preach unto them, and to teach them concerning the things pertaining to the kingdom of God." (Mosiah 18:16-18)

In the Bible, priests came from the tribe of Levi and worked in and around the tabernacle of God. This was needed during the time of the laws of Moses. It is written, "and thou shalt gird them with girdles, Aaron and his sons, and put the bonnets on them: and the priest's office shall be theirs for a perpetual statute: and thou shalt consecrate Aaron and his sons. And thou shalt cause a bullock to be brought before the tabernacle of the congregation: and Aaron and his sons shall put their hands upon the head of the bullock." (Exodus 29:9,10) Christ's church wasn't in existence at that time. This changed once Jesus came to earth. It is written, "and Simon Peter answered and said, Thou art the Christ, the Son of the living God. And Jesus answered and said unto him, Blessed art thou, Simon Barjona: for flesh and blood hath not revealed it unto thee, but my Father which is in heaven. And I say also unto thee, That thou art Peter, and upon this rock I will build my church; and the gates of hell shall not prevail against it." (Matthew 16:16-18)

Jesus's church was formed and is still on the earth today. It was founded in Israel and has spread around the globe to include all people, Jews and Gentiles. The people in the Book of Mormon are fiction. There was also no apostasy in Christ's church, for the gates of hell will not prevail against it. Do not trust the LDS Missionaries who say that there was a need for a restoration. They are telling people this, in order to lead them out of Christ's church and into a cult that does not save. It was never about religion that saved people, but a relationship with

Jesus that saves. The name on a church doesn't make it more true than others. Jesus isn't automatically for an organization just because they say they are for Him. What Jesus desires is for people to draw near unto Him, and then He will draw near unto you. His ways will become your ways and your beliefs will also be his. Allow the Lord Jesus to lead you like the priests of old did in times past. They were faithful to God in the tabernacle, as we ought to be faithful to Jesus now. Amen.

Let us pray:

Oh Lord, I pray that You will help unfold the truth to us. Many people think they have found the truth, but really they are deceived through false teachings that are not correct. I felt this way for over thirty years of my life, until the day a light bulb came on and everything changed. You revealed to me how false Mormonism really is, and I could not bear it any longer. If I was truly for You, then I would also be willing to lose friends, and even family members for a time. Surely, to leave what was comfortable for me, my wife, and my kids, was a lot of work at first. However, my relationship with You meant more than any other I formed on earth. Yes, God, If I live and die for the flesh and momentary pleasures, then I was never for You at all. For this reason, I put everything aside, and at the foot of the cross. Thank You for taking away the comforts of my old life for the sake of Your kingdom. I live for You and not the world. Conform me in Your ways. Move me to do what is right. Lead me this day and forever. I love You, Jesus. Amen.

Chapter 24

Priests Ordained From The Tribe Of Joseph

The Bible states that only the descendants of the tribe of Levi were made priests. These people served in the tabernacles of the old covenant. The Lord told Moses this while on Mount Sinai. It is written, "and the Lord spake unto Moses, saying, bring the tribe of Levi near, and present them before Aaron the priest, that they may minister unto him. And they shall keep his charge, and the charge of the whole congregation before the tabernacle of the congregation, to do the service of the tabernacle. And they shall keep all the instruments of the tabernacle of the congregation, and the charge of the children of Israel, to do the service of the tabernacle." (Numbers 3:5-8) Therefore, Levitical priests performed all the sacrificial offerings and other duties inside the tabernacle. God did not permit anyone else to perform these ordinances. However, with Jesus's death and resurrection, He became our last High Priest, and better tabernacle. We have no more need for temples made with hands.

The Book of Mormon would disagree when it comes to the priest's roles in God's tabernacle. It teaches that those of the tribe of Joseph were also priests. It is written, "and it came to pass that I, Nephi, did consecrate Jacob and Joseph, that they should be priests and teachers over the land of my people." (2 Nephi 5:26) These fictional characters are supposedly from the tribe of Joseph. Even the official LDS website acknowledges this. "A record of one group from the tribe of Ephraim that was led from Jerusalem to America about 600 B.C. This group's record is called the stick of Ephraim or Joseph, or the Book of Mormon." (Ephraim) Priests play a significant role in Mormon churches today. Men are believed to be from the tribe of Joseph, where they serve as priests and high priests. These are callings for boys at the age of 12 and older in the church. This goes against God's directives. Jesus is our high priest, and His believers are all under His royal priesthood. Also, the tribe of Levi no longer holds the priesthood anymore, for it is not necessary.

The Book of Mormon is said to be based on a group of people who came from Israel, specifically the tribe of Ephraim. If you recall, Ephraim was Joseph's son in Egypt. It is written, "a record of one group from the tribe of Ephraim that was led from Jerusalem to America about 600 B.C. This group's record is called the stick of Ephraim or Joseph, or the Book of Mormon." (Ephraim) All this is based on Ezekiel, chapter 37. Where it claims the stick of Joseph are people who came to America. It reads, "the word of the Lord came again unto me, saying, moreover, thou son of man, take thee one stick, and write upon it, For Judah, and for the children of Israel his companions: then take another stick, and write upon it, For Joseph, the stick of Ephraim and for all the house of Israel his companions: And join them one to another into one stick; and they shall become one in thine hand. And when the children of thy people shall speak unto thee, saying, Wilt thou not shew us what thou meanest by these?" (Ezekiel 37:15-18) There are two problems with how Mormons translate these verses, and we will discuss that next.

The two sticks are the kingdoms of Judah and Joseph. They were divided, but would soon be brought back together again. This passage is not about a people going to America. It is written, "and say unto them, Thus saith the Lord God; Behold, I will take the children of Israel from among the heathen, whither they be gone, and will gather them on every side, and bring them into their own land." (Ezekiel 37:21) The good news is that Israel did become one nation again. The bad news is that the stick of Joseph is not the Book of Mormon. Also, there is nothing about Ephraim as the LDS church claims in their book. It's about Manasseh. Alma, chapter 10 says this. It is written, "and Aminadi was a descendant of Nephi, who was the son of Lehi, who came out of the land of Jerusalem, who was a descendant of Manasseh, who was the son of Joseph who was sold into Egypt by the hands of his brethren." (Alma 10:3) Lastly, these priests were not from the tribe of Levi, but from Manasseh. This is a problem that people in the LDS people need to reconcile. Jesus is the answer and not religion. Amen.

Let us pray:

Oh Lord, I pray that many Mormons will come to faith. I know many of them personally, and it breaks my heart to know how deceived they really are. The Book of Mormon has many contradictions when compared to the Bible. People should reconsider what they have been taught. Thank You for helping me know what the Bible says. How our beliefs should not waver from what Your Word says. You've helped me understand that believing in something that contradicts what the Bible says is a no-go. So, I search the scriptures to make sure what I believe in comes from You and not man. Lord, I place the Bible above all books. Nothing can match what has been passed down from generation to generation with the writings of this book. It is the book to rule all books, for it comes from You, God. I know that many books have been written that contain different truths. But it is amazing to see a book like the Bible that is true from the first page to the end. I can trust everything that was written down in Your holy Word. The Bible is true. Lord, help the LDS people know this also. I love You, Jesus. Amen.

Chapter 25

Saved After All We Can Do

Christians believe that we are saved by grace alone, faith alone. This is also taught in the Book of Mormon. It is written, "that it is only in and through the grace of God that ye are saved." (2 Nephi 10:24) This verse teaches that our faith alone saves us, not saved after all we can do, or saved because of our works. This verse is often ignored by Mormons. This is because the verse contradicts another verse in this same book. An apostle in the Mormon church makes mention of it. It is written, "I am profoundly grateful for the principle of saving grace. Many people think they need only confess that Jesus is the Christ and then they are saved by grace alone. We cannot be saved by grace alone, for we know that it is by grace that we are saved, after all we can do, 2 Nephi 25:23." (President James E. Faust, "The Atonement: Our Greatest Hope," Ensign, Nov. 2001, 18.) This is a works-based salvation. Another article says this. "We believe that through the Atonement of Christ, all mankind may be saved, by obedience to the laws and ordinances of the Gospel." (Tough Topics: Are You Saved by Grace or Works?)

While the Book of Mormon and Mormon teachings collide with each other when it comes to salvation, the Bible is clear on the topic. That Salvation comes through our faith in Jesus, not the works that are produced from our faith. Paul taught, "for by grace are ye saved through faith; and that not of yourselves: it is the gift of God: Not of works, lest any man should boast. For we are his workmanship, created in Christ Jesus unto good works, which God hath before ordained that we should walk in them." (Ephesians 2:8-10) Paul talks about good works that God would manifest in our lives. This occurs when we look to Jesus, and He saves us through our faith in Him. We allow God to guide us by the Holy Spirit, which allows Him to showcase His gifts in our lives towards others. Paul also said this. "That if thou shalt confess with thy mouth the Lord Jesus, and shalt believe in thine heart that God hath raised him from the dead, thou shalt be saved. For with the heart man believeth unto righteousness; and with the mouth confession is made unto salvation." (Romans 10:9,10) Church ordinances don't save us, but our faith in Jesus alone does.

Looking at 2 Nephi, chapter 25, in the Book of Mormon, we learn a different story about how a person is saved. It is no longer faith alone in Jesus that saves us, but the works that are produced in our lives that saves us. It is written, "for we labor diligently to write, to persuade our children, and also our brethren, to believe in Christ, and to be reconciled to God; for we know that it is by grace that we are saved, after all we can do." (2 Nephi 25:23) My question about this verse is the following. Will people ever do enough to be saved if this is how salvation works? This shows that people rely on their works for salvation more than their faith in Jesus. On the other hand, the Bible teaches us that our faith alone in Jesus saves. Works are simply the fruits of our salvation, not what saves a person. So why is it that Mormons believe in a works-based salvation? It is because they want to be exalted to Godhood. Through doing their temple ordinances, they attempt to work their way to the Celestial kingdom in heaven. This is where they teach that people are exalted to Godhood as husband and wife. To reach the highest place in heaven, one must go through the temple. In these buildings, they get married, and continue performing rituals for the dead and themselves until death.

The Bible is clear that we cannot work our way to heaven. Anybody who thinks this is doing evil in God's sight. These man-made works are as filthy rags. Only through our faith in Jesus can a person be saved. Works come later on. Our faith is like a seed that eventually grows and matures. This is when we allow God to work in our lives. In all this, God still counts our faith for salvation, and not the works. It is written "for by grace are ye saved through faith; and that not of yourselves: it is the gift of God: Not of works, lest any man should boast." (Ephesians 2:8,9) This faith in Jesus is not dead but alive. This is why it produces works as a result of our faith. God's kingdom is full of spiritual giftings for true believers. These gifts come through faith in Jesus, and helps us grow and mature in the faith. This is being led by the Holy Spirit and doing as God says. After we have faith in Christ, our lives are transformed. We no longer do our own works, but God does the works in us. Give thanks to God for saving us through our continued faith in Jesus. He does the works in every believer. These are the fruits of our salvation. Amen.

Let us pray:

Oh Lord, I pray that people who say they love You will come to know the truth. It is one thing to say we love You, but another thing to do as You say. The truth is, most people are not led by the Holy Spirit and only do what their flesh desires. This is happening in many churches, like we see in Mormonism. The men wear shirts and ties, while the women wear modest dresses to church. They look very religious on the outside, but inwardly they are lost and without a shepherd. What their false prophets tell them, they acknowledge as Your truth and do it. Lord, it is sad knowing that I have family in this false religion. They are very hard-hearted when it comes to knowing anything different from what their church teaches. You have revealed to me that their works for the dead are an abomination in Your sight. The works inside their temples are truly wicked. They are filthy rags and nothing more. Lord, wake them up to the darkness that is ahead of them. I do not wish for anyone in this false religion to die and go to hell. Therefore, lead them to the truth through people in the faith, dreams, visions, and more. I trust in You, God. I love You, Lord. Amen.

Chapter 26

A Son Of King Zedekiah
Survived

The Book of Mormon states that a man named "Mulek" is the lone surviving son of King Zedekiah. However, after doing a simple word search for the man "Mulek" in all the Bible we find nothing. Even if he did exist and survived, then we would know about a son surviving the sword by the hand of the king of Babylon. This happened during the time of the prophet Jeremiah, when the king of Babylon killed Zedekiah's sons and gouged out his eyes. So, if there was a son that survived, wouldn't that be recorded in the Bible? Of course. Now, for you to understand what really happened to Zedekiah and His sons, let's turn to Jeremiah, chapter 39. It is written, "but the Chaldeans' army pursued after them, and overtook Zedekiah in the plains of Jericho: and when they had taken him, they brought him up to Nebuchadnezzar king of Babylon to Riblah in the land of Hamath, where he gave judgment upon him. Then the king of Babylon slew the sons of Zedekiah in Riblah before his eyes: also the king of Babylon slew all the nobles of Judah. Moreover he put out Zedekiah's eyes, and bound him with chains, to carry him to Babylon." (Jeremiah 39:5-7)

The Bible states that all the sons of King Zedekiah were killed. However, the Book of Mormon says a son survived. Both stories cannot be correct. There is no room for error. Therefore, the story of Mulek in the Book of Mormon cannot be trusted, for it denies what the Bible says. It is written, "and it came to pass that they became exceedingly rich, both the Lamanites and the Nephites; and they did have an exceeding plenty of gold, and of silver, and of all manner of precious metals, both in the land south and in the land north. Now the land south was called Lehi, and the land north was called Mulek, which was after the son of Zedekiah; for the Lord did bring Mulek into the land north, and Lehi into the land south." (Helaman 6:9,10) To believe this story of king Zedekiah and his surviving son, is to reject the validity of the Bible. And if we reject this story in Helaman, we must reject everything in the Book of Mormon as a whole. I am speaking the truth. This is just one of many contradictions in the Book of Mormon, which makes it false. What the Book of Mormon does is try to add details like this to the Biblical text.

There is irrefutable evidence that the Book of Mormon is false, and I will show you this today. Truly, "in the mouth of two or three witnesses shall every word be established." (2 Corinthians 13:1) Let's examine three chapters of the Bible and compare them with two different chapters in the Book of Mormon. Just know that the stories are vastly different stories when comparing the two books. In 2 Kings, chapter 25, and Jeremiah, chapters 39 and 52, we learn about the sons of Zedekiah, and how they were killed before the eyes of the king. King Nebuchadnezzar killed Zedekiah's sons in front of him and then blinded Zedekiah. Meanwhile, the Book of Mormon teaches a different story, where a son of Zedekiah escaped. The son is named "Mulek." The Book of Mormon says that he came to America with Lehi and his family. See for yourself how this is a huge contradiction to the Bible, and a smoking gun as to why the Book of Mormon cannot be trusted. These are the verses in the Bible that I am referring to...

"And the army of the Chaldees pursued after the king, and overtook him in the plains of Jericho: and all his army were scattered from him. So they took the king, and brought him up to the king of Babylon to Riblah; and they gave judgment upon him. And they slew the sons of Zedekiah before his eyes, and put out the eyes of Zedekiah, and bound him with fetters of brass, and carried him to Babylon. And in the fifth month, on the seventh day of the month, which is the nineteenth year of king Nebuchadnezzar king of Babylon, came Nebuzar-adan, captain of the guard, a servant of the king of Babylon, unto Jerusalem." (2 Kings 25:5-8)

"And it came to pass, that when Zedekiah the king of Judah saw them, and all the men of war, then they fled, and went forth out of the city by night, by the way of the king's garden, by the gate betwixt the two walls: and he went out the way of the plain. But the Chaldeans' army pursued after them, and overtook Zedekiah in the plains of Jericho: and when they had taken him, they brought him up to Nebuchadnezzar king of Babylon to Riblah in the land of Hamath, where he gave judgment upon him. Then the king of Babylon slew the sons of Zedekiah in Riblah before his eyes: also the king of Babylon slew all the nobles of Judah. Moreover he put out Zedekiah's eyes, and bound him with chains, to carry him to Babylon." (Jeremiah 39:4-7)

"But the army of the Chaldeans pursued after the king, and overtook Zedekiah in the plains of Jericho; and all his army was scattered from him. Then they took the king, and carried him up unto the king of Babylon to Riblah in the land of Hamath; where he gave judgment upon him. And the king of Babylon slew the sons of Zedekiah before his eyes: he slew also all the princes of Judah in Riblah. Then he put out the eyes of Zedekiah; and the king of Babylon bound him in chains, and carried him to Babylon, and put him in prison till the day of his death." (Jeremiah 52:8-11)

And now read the two chapters in the Book of Mormon that teach that one son escaped death and came to America. It comes from Helaman, chapters 6 and 8. These verses read....

"And it came to pass that they became exceedingly rich, both the Lamanites and the Nephites; and they did have an exceeding plenty of gold, and of silver, and of all manner of precious metals, both in the land south and in the land north. Now the land south was called Lehi, and the land north was called Mulek, which was after the son of Zedekiah; for the Lord did bring Mulek into the land north, and Lehi into the land south." (Helaman 6:9,10)

"And now will you dispute that Jerusalem was destroyed? Will ye say that the sons of Zedekiah were not slain, all except it were Mulek? Yea, and do ye not behold that the seed of Zedekiah are with us, and they were driven out of the land of Jerusalem? But behold, this is not all." (Helaman 8:21)

The Bible is clear that the sons of Zedekiah, king of Judah, was killed because of the king of Babylon. It was king Nebuchadnezzar that caused this to happen. Looking at the timeline in history, this happened around 587 B.C. In this same timeframe, a fictional group of people from the Book of Mormon left Israel to go to America. This strange book states that it is a wrong interpretation to say that all the sons were killed. Therefore, they lead people to believe that a man named "Mulek" survived the killing, being the son of Zedekiah. The Bible disagrees and says, "and the army of the Chaldees pursued after the king, and overtook him in the plains of Jericho: and all his army were scattered from him. So, they took the king, and brought him up to the king of Babylon to Riblah; and they gave judgment upon him. And they slew the sons of Zedekiah before his eyes, and put out the eyes of Zedekiah, and bound him with fetters of brass, and carried him to Babylon." (2 Kings 25:5-7)

There must be two witnesses for God's Word to be established. We can trust a specific doctrine or teaching because the Bible teaches the same thing in more than one place. This is the case with the sons of Zedekiah. These young men were killed before Nebuchadnezzar, the king of Babylon. This is when their father was captured by the army of the Chaldeans, and later on slain. It was soon afterward that King Zedekiah had his eyes removed by the enemy. This is the teaching that is found in 2 Kings 25:5-8, Jeremiah 39:4-7, and Jeremiah 52:8-11. I am seeing three different accounts in the Bible that teaches us the same thing about the sons of Zedekiah. However, the Book of Mormon disagrees with these verses. As we've already seen, a son survived in Joseph's book.

The Book of Mormon teaches that a son of Zedekiah, named "Mulek", survived and went to America. But what will you believe? Just think this through. The Book of Mormon cannot be of God if the story of Zedekiah in the Bible is true. All his sons were either killed or not. If you are a Mormon, you must make a choice today about what you will believe in. The Bible or the Book of Mormon. You cannot believe in both books since their stories are different regarding the sons of Zedekiah. If you simply ponder upon both stories, you will see how they contradict. God led me to discuss this fact with members of the Mormon faith. This caused their false beliefs to unravel before my eyes. The Book of Mormon cannot be of God if it is in conflict with the Bible. In this instance, the Book of Mormon tells us that "Mulek" went to America, and the Bible says all his sons were killed. The contradiction is clear. The Book of Mormon is not of God.

It is in the Book of Mormon that we hear about this contradiction. In Helaman 8, it reads, "and now will you dispute that Jerusalem was destroyed? Will ye say that the sons of Zedekiah were not slain, all except it were Mulek? Yea, and do ye not behold that the seed of Zedekiah are with us, and they were driven out of the land of Jerusalem? But behold, this is not all. (Helaman 8:21) And there you go. The Book of Mormon teaches things that are contrary to what the Bible has already said are true. It doesn't just do this here but in dozens of other places all over this man-made book. You can hear the voices of Joseph Smith and the early founders of Mormonism written all over this book. Contrary to what the Book of Mormon claims, a son of King Zedekiah did not escape his death. He also did not come to the Americas. For this reason, people should stop reading the Book of Mormon altogether, lest they disbelieve the Bible more and more. This is my prayer for all Mormons.

People need to make a choice. Either believe what the Bible says is true or the Book of Mormon. You cannot believe both books and feel good about yourself. This is especially true when the stories of Zedekiah's sons do not line up with each other. Therefore, make a choice as to what book is true. Both books cannot be true. They do not complement each other at all. These stories collide with one another, and this should be a big red flag. This specific contradiction would not exist if the Book of Mormon was another testament of Jesus Christ. The proof is in the pudding. Think this through and put aside what you have been taught concerning the Book of Mormon. Consider it to be false. This is not an accusation that can easily be put to rest when looking at the outcome of the sons of Zedekiah.

Not too long ago I knocked on a door where a young man at the age of 18 answered. My friend and I in the faith were knocking on doors and happened to find him that day. He was a Mormon getting ready to go on his mission, where his dad was a Bishop in his ward. In the time we had together, I mentioned the story of Zedekiah and how all his sons were killed. How the Bible supports this teaching, but the Book of Mormon does not. Seeing how a son supposedly survived. I then asked him if he could believe in the Book of Mormon and the Bible if what the Bible says is true. He said "No". He would have to choose one story over the other and could not believe in both books. We then talked to him for the next hour and a half. His heart was more than open to receive the truth of God that day. I am grateful that He allowed the Lord to speak to His heart. Lastly, just because the Book of Mormon is shown to be false, don't give up on the Bible. It is still true, along with Jesus being God. Amen.

Let us pray:

Oh Lord, help Mormons learn to trust the Bible more and more each day. To distrust fictional books like the Book of Mormon, and trust in You instead. If only they would read the Bible daily and stop reading their Book of Mormon, things would change for the better. Lord, I am praying that Mormons will do this and come to You, Jesus, for salvation. To not go down the road of atheism, for You still save, and the Bible is still true. They believe that the more they bear their testimony about their church being true, the more it will help keep the faith. This is the spirit of the devil causing them to be firm in their false beliefs, instead of being open to Your truth. Lord, I love these people, but to get through to them is so difficult. Thankfully, we have the freedom to share the truth of God on social media, websites, and books to help them. I may not be able to reach many Mormons in person, but online is where amazing things are happening. Thank You, Lord, for the hundreds of people that have already resigned. I give You glory and praise. I love You, Jesus. Amen.

Chapter 27

The Trinity

The Mormon Godhead makes up the Father, Jesus, and the Holy Spirit. They are each God, making up three Gods or Beings in total. This is odd to see since their own Book of Mormon teaches the opposite. You may be surprised but the Trinity is taught. It is written, "and now, behold, my beloved brethren, this is the way; and there is none other way nor name given under heaven whereby man can be saved in the kingdom of God. And now, behold, this is the doctrine of Christ, and the only and true doctrine of the Father, and of the Son, and of the Holy Ghost, which is one God, without end. Amen." (2 Nephi 31:21) How interesting. What lesson did this verse just teach us? Answer: The Holy Trinity. That God the Father, Jesus the Son, and the Holy Spirit are three persons in one God. They work together in perfect unity. Too bad this is not taught in the Mormon Church. The evidence is in their own book, but they deny it. Instead, they make up a God to be what they want, which is three individual Gods.

This teaching of the trinity is biblical. John taught, "for there are three that bear record in heaven, the Father, the Word, and the Holy Ghost: and these three are one. And there are three that bear witness in earth, the Spirit, and the water, and the blood: and these three agree in one." (1 John 5:7,8) So the Father, Jesus, and the Holy Spirit are three persons, but still one. These verses are similar to what I quoted in the Book of Mormon. I am not saying that the Book of Mormon is true, but that Joseph Smith once believed in the Trinity. However, the Mormon church has shunned the Trinity doctrine and calls it heresy. The Bible says there is only one God, and they deny this also. One example comes from the book of Isaiah. It reads, "remember the former things of old: for I am God, and there is none else; I am God, and there is none like me." (Isaiah 46:9) As there is only one God, this confirms the Trinity is true. We may not totally understand how God works, but we have faith in Him nonetheless.

Problems begin when the Trinity is spoken against, and the Mormon Godhood is accepted. Instead of believing that the Father, Son, and Holy Spirit are one God, people now believe they are individually God. This makes three Gods in the Godhead. Christians believe that they are three persons in one being, who is God. Mormons would disagree and say they are separate beings and three Gods. On their official church website, LDS teach this. It reads, "like many Christians, we believe in God the Father, His Son Jesus Christ, and the Holy Spirit. However, we don't believe in the traditional concept of the Trinity. We believe that the Father, the Son, and the Holy Ghost are three separate beings who are one in purpose." (Do Members of The Church of Jesus Christ of Latter-day Saints Believe in the Trinity) How interesting they speak against the Trinity, while contradicting their own Book of Mormon. We see the Trinity in the following verse.

It is written, "and now, behold, my beloved brethren, this is the way; and there is none other way nor name given under heaven whereby man can be saved in the kingdom of God. And now, behold, this is the doctrine of Christ, and the only and true doctrine of the Father, and of the Son, and of the Holy Ghost, which is one God, without end. Amen." (2 Nephi 31:21)

Let's read from 1 John, chapter 5, once again. It reads, "for there are three that bear record in heaven, the Father, the Word, and the Holy Ghost: and these three are one. And there are three that bear witness in earth, the Spirit, and the water, and the blood: and these three agree in one." (1 John 5:7,8) The Father, Jesus, and the Holy Spirit are three persons in one God just as the Jews believe in one God. James even said this when he wrote, "thou believest that there is one God; thou doest well: the devils also believe, and tremble." (James 2:19) This agrees with the teachings of Isaiah. It is written, "fear ye not, neither be afraid: have not I told thee from that time, and have declared it? ye are even my witnesses. Is there a God beside me? yea, there is no God; I know not any." (Isaiah 44:8) Therefore, there is only one God. This is because the Father is Spirit, and He and the Holy Spirit dwell perfectly with the Son. Speaking of the Father, Jesus said, "God is a Spirit: and they that worship him must worship him in spirit and in truth." (John 4:24) Therefore, we hold to the Trinity. This doctrine is not man-made, but the description and doctrines are found in the Bible.

The Book of Mormon teaches that God the Father, the Son, and the Holy Spirit are one God, like unto the Trinity. However, this contradicts their belief in the Godhead. In Alma, chapter 44, it teaches the following about the Trinity. It is written, "now, this restoration shall come to all, both old and young, both bond and free, both male and female, both the wicked and the righteous; and even there shall not so much as a hair of their heads be lost; but every thing shall be restored to its perfect frame, as it is now, or in the body, and shall be brought and be arraigned before the bar of Christ the Son, and God the Father, and the Holy Spirit, which is one Eternal God, to be judged according to their works, whether they be good or whether they be evil." (Alma 11:44) What we just read is the Trinity spoken of in the Bible. How the Father, Son, and Holy Spirit are one God. These three bear record in heaven. The Father leads the Son, as the Holy Ghost leads us into all truth. This happens since the Father and Holy Spirit are Spirit. They are then able to lead and guide our lives.

Here is the official doctrine of the Mormon church, which contradicts their own Book of Mormon and the Bible. "The true doctrine of the Godhead was lost in the apostasy that followed the Savior's mortal ministry and the deaths of His Apostles. This doctrine began to be restored when 14-year- old Joseph Smith received his First Vision (see Joseph Smith—History 1:17). "From the Prophet's account of the First Vision and from his other teachings, we know that the members of the Godhead are three separate beings. The Father and the Son have tangible bodies of flesh and bones, and the Holy Ghost is a personage of spirit (see Doctrine and Covenants 130:22)." (Godhead) This teaching is false. The Father is a Spirit and this is why He is able to dwell in the Son. Jesus said, "believest thou not that I am in the Father, and the Father in me? the words that I speak unto you I speak not of myself: but the Father that dwelleth in me, he doeth the works." (John 14:10) Lastly, the Trinity is from God as Paul also spoke of. It is written, "the grace of the Lord Jesus Christ, and the love of God, and the communion of the Holy Ghost, be with you all. Amen." (2

Corinthians 13:14) Who will you believe? Mormon doctrine or the Bible?

In 3 Nephi, chapter 11, we find the teaching of the Trinity being taught. Jesus is supposedly speaking, as He recently touched down in America. In this account, Joseph Smith adds flare to the story to make it sound real. It might sound interesting on paper until we look at the verse in detail. It is written, "and after this manner shall ye baptize in my name; for behold, verily I say unto you, that the Father, and the Son, and the Holy Ghost are one; and I am in the Father, and the Father in me, and the Father and I are one." (3 Nephi 11:27) From this verse I see three persons that are said to be one. It doesn't say one in purpose. The phrase, "the Father, and the Son, and the Holy Ghost are one" comes from 1 John 5:7. It reads, "for there are three that bear record in heaven, the Father, the Word, and the Holy Ghost: and these three are one." (1 John 5:7) This is the Trinity being taught. Where the Father, Son, and Holy Spirit exist as three different persons in one God. The Father is not the Son or the Holy Spirit and vice versa. However, Mormons would disagree with this interpretation of the verse. Therefore, they add "one in purpose" when it says "one".

This Jesus figure also said that "I am in the Father, and the Father in me". This comes from John, chapter 14. This passage reads, "believest thou not that I am in the Father, and the Father in me? the words that I speak unto you I speak not of myself: but the Father that dwelleth in me, he doeth the works. Believe me that I am in the Father, and the Father in me: or else believe me for the very works' sake." (John 14:10,11) As Christians, we use 1 John 5:7 and John 14:10,11 as proof texts for the Trinity. How interesting that we see the same teachings in the Book of Mormon, but still reject the Trinity. Those who are LDS will say that they are one in purpose and not one God. But how do Mormons deal with Jesus saying the Father dwells in Him? This is clearly talking about the Father's Spirit dwelling in the Son, which makes Him Spirit. This is a contradiction to Mormon teachings, not the Bible. The question I have is why don't the Mormon people believe what their own book teaches. I am not saying the Book of Mormon is true, but this is interesting to see them add to their book so it fits their belief system.

The doctrine of the trinity is taught in the Bible. Surprisingly, it is in the Book of Mormon also. I am not saying the Book of Mormon is from God, but it is interesting that it teaches this core Christian doctrine. It is odd, however, to see Mormons hate the doctrine of the trinity when their own book speaks of it loud and clear. I wonder what they think when they read verses in their Book of Mormon that refer to the Trinity. I am speaking of 2 Nephi 31:21, Alma 11:44, 3 Nephi 11:27,35,36, and Mormon 7:7. These verses have one thing in common and that is that the Father, Son, and Holy Spirit are one. Not once do the verses say, "one in purpose". I've spoken of the other verses except for the one in 3 Nephi. Let's read it now to see if it speaks of the trinity also. it is written, "verily, verily, I say unto you, that this is my doctrine, and I bear record of it from the Father; and whoso believeth in me believeth in the Father also; and unto him will the Father bear record of me, for he will visit him with fire and with the Holy Ghost. And thus will the Father bear record of me, and the Holy Ghost will bear record unto him of the Father and me; for the Father, and I, and the Holy Ghost are one." (3 Nephi 11:35,36) Therefore, the Father, Son, and Holy Spirit are one. I am not adding to these verses by saying one in purpose, the same way I do with the Bible.

When Mormons see the phrase, "the Father, Son, and the Holy Spirit are one", they see "one in purpose". It is written, "like many Christians, we believe in God the Father, His Son Jesus Christ, and the Holy Spirit. However, we don't believe in the traditional concept of the Trinity. We believe that the Father, the Son, and the Holy Ghost are three separate beings who are one in purpose." "We call them the Godhead." (Do Members of The Church of Jesus Christ of Latter-day Saints Believe in the Trinity?) The Godhead is taught in the Bible. It is written, "beware lest any man spoil you through philosophy and vain deceit, after the tradition of men, after the rudiments of the world, and not after Christ. For in him dwelleth all the fulness of the Godhead bodily." (Colossians 2:8,9) This is speaking of Christ's body, of which the Father's Spirit dwells. Jesus said, "believest thou not that I am in the Father, and the Father in me? the words that I speak unto you I speak not of myself: but the Father that dwelleth in me, he doeth the works." (John 14:10) Lastly, John wrote, "for there are three that bear record in heaven, the Father, the Word, and the Holy Ghost: and these three are one. " (1 John 5:7) God is one, not one in purpose.

The teaching of the Trinity has been popular among Christians throughout the centuries, and since Jesus was on earth. It makes sense that it is in the Book of Mormon. It is written, "and he hath brought to pass the redemption of the world, whereby he that is found guiltless before him at the judgment day hath it given unto him to dwell in the presence of God in his kingdom, to sing ceaseless praises with the choirs above, unto the Father, and unto the Son, and unto the Holy Ghost, which are one God, in a state of happiness which hath no end." (Mormon 7:7) So three persons in one God, or one being. However, the Mormon church doesn't believe this. They say, "the Trinity of traditional Christianity is referred to as the Godhead by members of The Church of Jesus Christ of Latter-day Saints. Like other Christians, Latter-day Saints believe in the Father, the Son and the Holy Spirit (or

Holy Ghost). Yet, Church teachings about the Godhead differ from those of traditional Christianity. For example, while some believe the three members of the Trinity are of one substance, Latter-day Saints believe they are three physically separate beings, but fully one in love, purpose and will." (Godhead)

Joseph Smith once believed in the trinity. This is why the teachings are found all throughout the Book of Mormon. The Mormon church may not believe in the Trinity, but their early beliefs included it. It is also taught in their Book of Mormon. Speaking of the Trinity, the Bible says, "and God said, Let us make man in our image, after our likeness: and let them have dominion over the fish of the sea, and over the fowl of the air, and over the cattle, and over all the earth, and over every creeping thing that creepeth upon the earth." (Genesis 1:26) The "us" in this context is Elohim, being one God in a plural nature. This being the Father, the Son, and the Holy Spirit. It is written, "in the beginning was the Word, and the Word was with God, and the Word was God." (John 1:1) Jesus said, "go ye therefore, and teach all nations, baptizing them in the name of the Father, and of the Son, and of the Holy Ghost." (Matthew 28:19) All three being one God. John said, "for there are three that bear record in heaven, the Father, the Word, and the Holy Ghost: and these three are one." (1 John 5:7) Therefore, the Trinity is Biblical as the definition is found in scripture. Amen.

Let us pray:

Oh Lord and my God, hear me now as I call upon Your Name. Father, Son, and Holy Spirit, I worship You. You are God, three in one. You deserve our praise, glory, and honor. You are mighty to save, Jesus, and I am grateful that You have come into my life. You have saved a wretch like me, and I am so grateful. I don't deserve Your love, but You show it just the same. In my tears, did You come and wipe them all away. You are the bearer of joy and continue to remove all the sadness from my heart. I have been down and depressed at times in my life, and You always came through, while bringing me peace and comfort. I never knew how much I needed You in my life until now. My life may not be perfect, but in You presence, I am much better off. This world is dark, and I need You every moment. I still have some pretty rough days, but You continue to swoop in and carry me when I am unable to walk on my own. Lord, because I have breath, You I give You praise. I am truly alive because of You. Thank You for trusting in me as Your servant, and witness on this earth. Help me to achieve the things that You desire for my life. I love You, Lord. You are my God and my King. I worship You. Amen.

Chapter 28

Worship Jesus

As Christians, we worship Jesus. But what about the Mormon people, do they do the same? If not, then why? They are called to worship Jesus in the Book of Mormon, although their church leaders would disagree. It is written, "and now behold, I say unto you that the right way is to believe in Christ, and deny him not; and Christ is the Holy One of Israel; wherefore ye must bow down before him, and worship him with all your might, mind, and strength, and your whole soul; and if ye do this ye shall in nowise be cast out." (2 Nephi 25:29) Other places in the Book of Mormon show people worshiping Jesus. However, the current Mormon teachings say that God the Father, and Him alone should be worshiped, not the Son. Bruce R Mcconkie, one of the 12 Apostles, said this. "We worship the Father and him only and no one else. We do not worship the Son, and we do not worship the Holy Ghost". (Our Relationship with the Lord) The lds.org website agrees with this statement. "God the Father is the Supreme Being in whom we believe and whom we worship." (God The Father)

As you can see by the statements from the Mormon church, they don't agree with worshiping Jesus. Therefore, the Mormon prophets and their book cannot be trusted. This leads us to believe the Mormons are not led by God. They cannot have it both ways. To be divided in doctrine is wrong and not of God. Therefore, the Mormon prophets are false, and their church is false also. On that note, let us clear up the confusion. Turn with me to the true Word of God, the Bible, that talks about worshiping Jesus. In Matthew, chapter 28, we learn how Jesus accepts worship. It reads, "and they departed quickly from the sepulchre with fear and great joy; and did run to bring his disciples word. And as they went to tell his disciples, behold, Jesus met them, saying, All hail. And they came and held him by the feet, and worshipped him." (Matthew 28:8,9) As this happened, Jesus did not say, do not do this, but accepted it. This happened all throughout His ministry. When people bowed down before Jesus, He accepted the worship. People saw Jesus as we see Him now. He is our Lord, our God, and King. The promised Messiah.

In the same chapter of Matthew, it says the following. "Then the eleven disciples went away into Galilee, into a mountain where Jesus had appointed them. And when they saw him, they worshipped him: but some doubted." (Matthew 28:16,17) As you can see here, as people saw the resurrected Lord, they could not help but worship Him. They fell at His feet in worship and He accepted it. Not once did He tell people to stop. However, when John attempted to worship an angel, the angel said stop. It is written, "see thou do it not: for I am thy fellow servant, and of thy brethren the prophets, and of them which keep the sayings of this book: worship God." (Revelation 22:9) Since Jesus and the Father are both considered God, then to worship them both is fine. Let us read in Jesus's own words how he is the

God of Abraham, after being asked if he had seen Him. Jesus said, "Before Abraham was, I am." (John 8:58) Therefore, as Christians, we stick with what the Bible teaches about worshiping Jesus. Mormons, however, cannot agree, for their doctrines of worshiping the Father only are contradictory to what the Book of Mormon and Bible say.

I have noticed that Mormons read their Book of Mormon, but don't do what it says. I am not saying that this book is of God, but what it is crazy that they hold to this book being the most correct book on earth. In so doing, they don't believe in a lot of what it says. Namely, the Trinity that is found in 2 Nephi 31:21 and Mormon 7:7, and also to worship Jesus in 2 Nephi 25:29. Let's read this verse again. It is written, "and now behold, I say unto you that the right way is to believe in Christ, and deny him not; and Christ is the Holy One of Israel; wherefore ye must bow down before him, and worship him with all your might, mind, and strength, and your whole soul; and if ye do this ye shall in nowise be cast out." (2 Nephi 25:29) This verse contradicts what Bruce R. McConkie said. It is written, "we do not worship the Son, and we do not worship the Holy Ghost. I know perfectly well what the scriptures say about worshipping Christ and Jehovah, but they are speaking in an entirely different sense—the sense of standing in awe and being reverentially grateful to him who has redeemed us. Worship in the true and saving sense is reserved for God the first, the Creator." (Our Relationship with the Lord, 1982)

The truth is, Jesus was worshiped by different people during His ministry on earth. He also never told them to stop. It is written, "and as they went to tell his disciples, behold, Jesus met them, saying, All hail. And they came and held him by the feet, and worshipped him. Then said Jesus unto them, Be not afraid: go tell my brethren that they go into Galilee, and there shall they see me." (Matthew 28:9,10) "Then the eleven disciples went away into Galilee, into a mountain where Jesus had appointed them. And when they saw him, they worshipped him: but some doubted. And Jesus came and spake unto them, saying, All power is given unto me in heaven and in earth." (Matthew 28:16-18) Lastly, every person will bow before Jesus, if not in this life. It is written, "that at the name of Jesus every knee should bow, of things in heaven, and things in earth, and things under the earth; And that every tongue should confess that Jesus Christ is Lord, to the glory of God the Father." (Philippians 2:10,11) True Christians worship Jesus and the Father. This means praying to the Father or the Son. It is sad to see Mormons deny worshiping Jesus. This contradicts their own teachings in the Book of Mormon. Amen.

Let us pray:

Oh Lord, help us to know Your will and follow after it also. You are God, Jesus, and many people will say this but do nothing to show their worship. It is sad to hear from people that they only worship the Father and not You. Do they not know that You are worthy of our praise also, Jesus? How that every knee will bow down before You one way or another in this life or the next. As for me, I've already made my decision to follow You completely and to make You Lord of my life. People can persecute me, but this will not deter me from following You, Lord. I bestow upon You, Jesus, glory and praise. I worship You now and forever. You are the Son of Man, who came into this world, in order to save us from our sins. Thank You, God. Because of the cross, your blood has covered me. For this reason, I tell everyone I can about You and Your payment for sins on the cross. Many people get this wrong while adding Gethsemane to the atonement. In these false beliefs, every person will know in death and judgment that You died for our sins. Forgive me, Lord. Wash me clean from all my iniquities. I love You, Jesus. Amen.

Chapter 29

Book Of Mormon: Examining 5 Things

The Book of Mormon (BOM) is said to be the most correct book on earth, according to Mormons. For that reason, let us put it to the test to see if it complements or goes against the teachings of the Bible. Here are just 5 things that we know about and is taught from its pages:

1. The Book of Mormon is another testament or gospel of Jesus Christ. It is taught that it is the most correct book on earth.

2. Before Jesus's Birth, the Book of Mormon people were using the names "Christ", "Jesus", or "Jesus Christ".

3. Before Jesus's Birth, the Book of Mormon people were being forgiven by the blood of Jesus.

4. Jesus was born in Jerusalem.

5. Melchisedec had a father and mother.

Let us now compare these Book of Mormon teachings with the Bible.

1.

BOM Teaching: The Book of Mormon is another testament or gospel of Jesus Christ. It is taught that it is the most correct book on earth. Joseph Smith said, "I told the brethren that the Book of Mormon was the most correct of any book on earth, and the keystone of our religion, and a man would get nearer to God by abiding by its precepts, than by any other book" (History of the Church, 4:461)

Bible Teaching: Beware of another gospel different from the Bible. "I marvel that ye are so soon removed from him that called you into the grace of Christ unto another gospel: Which is not another; but there be some that trouble you, and would pervert the gospel of Christ. But though we, or an angel from heaven, preach any other gospel unto you than that which we have preached unto you, let him be accursed." (Galatians 1:6-8)

2.

BOM Teaching: Before Jesus's Birth, the Book of Mormon people were using the names "Christ", "Jesus", or "Jesus Christ". His name is found all throughout the Book of Mormon timeframe, especially before His birth.

Bible Teaching: It wasn't until right before Jesus's birth that someone used the name "Christ" or "Jesus". Mary was told that her Son would be called Jesus by an angel. It is written, "And, behold, thou shalt conceive in thy womb, and bring forth a son, and shalt call his name Jesus." (Luke 1:31) Jesus's name first appeared with His genealogy and birth in Matthew, chapter 1. It is written, "And Jacob begat Joseph the husband of Mary, of whom was born Jesus, who is called Christ." (Matthew 1:16) "Now the birth of Jesus Christ was on this wise: When as his mother Mary was espoused to Joseph, before they came together, she was found with child of the Holy Ghost." (Matthew 1:18)

3.

BOM Teaching: Before Jesus's Birth, the Book of Mormon people were forgiven by the blood of Jesus. It is written, "and now, it came to pass that when king Benjamin had made an end of speaking the words which had been delivered unto him by the angel of the Lord, that he cast his eyes round about on the multitude, and behold they had fallen to the earth, for the fear of the Lord had come upon them. And they had viewed themselves in their own carnal state, even less than the dust of the earth. And they all cried aloud with one voice, saying: O have mercy, and apply the atoning blood of Christ that we may receive forgiveness of our sins, and our hearts may be purified; for we believe in Jesus Christ, the Son of God, who created heaven and earth, and all things; who shall come down among the children of men." (Mosiah 4:1,2) (124 B.C)

Bible Teaching: Jesus came to earth in order to save us from our sins. He knew from the beginning that He would ultimately be raised up on a cross. Because He died for our sins, we are forgiven and sanctified by the blood of Jesus. It is written, "and you, being dead in your sins and the uncircumcision of your flesh, hath he quickened together with him, having forgiven you all trespasses; Blotting out the handwriting of ordinances that was against us, which was contrary to us, and took it out of the way, nailing it to his cross." (Colossians

2:13,14) "For Christ also hath once suffered for sins, the just for the unjust, that he might bring us to God, being put to death in the flesh, but quickened by the Spirit." (1 Peter 3:18)

4.

BOM Teaching: Jesus was born in Jerusalem. It is written, "and behold, he shall be born of Mary, at Jerusalem which is the land of our forefathers, she being a virgin, a precious and chosen vessel, who shall be overshadowed and conceive by the power of the Holy Ghost, and bring forth a son, yea, even the Son of God." (Alma 7:10)

Bible Teaching: Jesus was born in Bethlehem. It is written, "but thou, Bethlehem Ephratah, though thou be little among the thousands of Judah, yet out of thee shall he come forth unto me that is to be ruler in Israel; whose goings forth have been from of old, from everlasting." (Micah 5:2) "Now when Jesus was born in Bethlehem of Judaea in the days of Herod the king, behold, there came wise men from the east to Jerusalem" (Matthew 2:1)

5.

BOM Teaching: Melchisedec had a father and mother. It is written, "but Melchizedek having exercised mighty faith, and received the office of the high priesthood according to the holy order of God, did preach repentance unto his people. And behold, they did repent; and Melchizedek did establish peace in the land in his days; therefore he was called the prince of peace, for he was the king of Salem; and he did reign under his father." (Alma 13:18)

Bible Teaching: Melchisedec had no father or mother. "For this Melchisedec, king of Salem, priest of the most high God, who met Abraham returning from the slaughter of the kings, and blessed him;

To whom also Abraham gave a tenth part of all; first being by interpretation King of righteousness, and after that also King of Salem, which is, King of peace; Without father, without mother, without descent, having neither beginning of days, nor end of life; but made like unto the Son of God; abideth a priest continually." (Hebrews 7:1-3)

As you can see above, it is easy to see that the Book of Mormon is not on par with the Bible. These 5 teachings alone are contrary to God's Word. Therefore, it teaches things that go against God's Word and should be rejected. Any religious book that does not compliment the Biblical texts is of man and cannot be trusted. Read the Bible, lest you be led astray also. Anyone that has read this message and is in Mormonism, please let it sink in. I pray that you no longer continue in a religion with man-made teachings.

Let us pray:

Oh Lord, deliver the Mormon people out of bondage. You have shown me how false the Book of Mormon is, and I pray that others will also experience this. I have so many family members that are stuck in this false religion. They are unaware that they are on the path to destruction. God, I have tried to reach them and many other people in the Mormon cult, but only few people have listened. This has caused me to be saddened by their carnal and wicked state. I know that only people who know You are saved. There is only destruction for people who work their way to heaven, instead of going through You alone, Jesus. Deliver those who are humble into Your loving arms. As they question their beliefs, give them over to what the Bible says. You can do all things. I love You, Lord. I offer You my highest praise and glory. Amen.

Conclusion

I have addressed various contradictions in the Book of Mormon, but my intention was never to promote atheism. Rather, my goal was to emphasize the importance of coming to Jesus for salvation. The Bible is our foundation for truth. That is why I tried and tested different verses of the Book of Mormon with the Biblical text. The Bible is our foundation for truth. I read the Book of Mormon, as LDS Missionaries have asked me to. I then went through the chapters in this book and began to see some things I agreed with and other things I did not. This was only the case since I used the Bible as my form of reference. I compared verses with the Biblical text, and it was easy to see how the Book of Mormon is not of God. I was glad to find parts in the text that talk about the lake of fire, the Trinity, worshiping Jesus, and more. It was interesting to see that Mormons are against those teachings when their book is for them. I am not adding to the Book of Mormon by saying this.

There were other verses I would disagree with as the teachings contradict the theology taught in the Bible. How we are not saved by faith alone in Jesus, people need to be baptized to be saved, Gentiles are not the lost sheep, and more. These are man-made doctrines that go against the Bible. I have addressed many other things that are not Biblical, of which the Book of Mormon teaches. Therefore, it is right to put it aside and stop reading it. At this point, consider that the Bible is still true. Too many people stop believing in Jesus after leaving the Mormon church and this is sad. So, after acknowledging that the Book of Mormon is false, what does a person do from here? My prayer is that people will give their lives to Jesus and be saved. If only people would deny what is false and allow Jesus to be their teacher, God can move in their lives. Humility is required for this. Our faith in Jesus produces good works. The works we produce without God are filthy rags in his sight. So, allow the Holy Spirit to lead you.

Our journey on earth may come to an end today. This is a harsh reality that we all must think about. This life is short and when everything is all said and done, our spirits will either go to a place called paradise or hell. You might be asking, but what does this have to do with this book? It has everything to do with it. I prayed for people to come to Jesus in every chapter and meant it. If you are a Mormon, then I was praying for you also. The LDS church may not be true, but Jesus is still God, and the Bible is still His Word. If you allow Him into your life, you will be forgiven through the blood he shed for us on the cross. There have always been false teachers that have tried to drive people away from God and His truth. But today is the day of salvation. Set aside the Book of Mormon and allow the Lord to be Your teacher. It is not about religion but a relationship with Jesus that saves. If Jesus doesn't know you, then you are not welcome in His kingdom. Come to know the Lord and He will lead you safely home. Amen.

Testimonial

I am the granddaughter of Latter-Day Saints who were married in the Salt Lake City Temple. I have friends who are LDS and are active in their ward and temple. I thought that their faith would meet the criteria laid out in God's Word for salvation. Since reading messages from Paul Gee's website (christvm.com) and others, my thoughts have changed. In the process of editing this book I've learned so much. For instance, I've learned how the foundation of Mormonism, as revealed in the Book of Mormon, is built on sand. There is no evidence for it, and the Jesus in the Book of Mormon is not the same as the Bible. I once preferred to continue in my world of denial. Now, I appreciate learning the truth. Joseph Smith claimed that the Book of Mormon was "the most perfect book". Its title is Another Testament of Jesus Christ. If so, I would expect it to mirror the teachings of the Bible. It doesn't.

The Book of Mormon should meet the test of authenticity in the areas of history, archaeology, and science. Nothing to date has shown this. I can only conclude that the Book of Mormon is fraudulent. When holding this book to the same standard as the Bible it is found wanting. Every chapter of Paul's book contains verses from the Bible and the Book of Mormon, where contradictions are seen. When comparing the verses in the two books, it is clear that there is a different Jesus. What he says and does in the Book of Mormon contradicts the true Jesus of the Bible. In reading through this book, there is undeniable proof of how the Book of Mormon contradicts the Bible. It leaves no doubt in my mind that the book claimed to be "Another Testament of Jesus Christ" is not.

Paul strengthens his argument by pointing out the inconsistencies between the doctrines of The Church of Jesus Christ of Latter-Day Saints and the teachings of their own book. So the question must be asked, "Do Mormons even believe in the Book of Mormon? Future converts are told to read it all the time, while the LDS missionaries don't even believe in certain verses. This doesn't make sense. Joseph Smith's claim that the Book of Mormon is 'the most perfect book" is crushed under the weight of evidence. By comparing the book's teachings to the Bible, Paul's work makes a unique contribution to the study of Mormonism. It reveals some of the glaring problems found in the Book of Mormon. In conclusion, Paul has made a rock-solid case for the Book of Mormon being not of God. It is nothing more than a figment of Joseph Smith's imagination and a document of plagiarism.

- Geri Ehrlich

Hope After
Mormonism

Out of love and respect, I want you to know that it is necessary to leave what is false behind. There is hope for people who are willing to give up things for the sake of Jesus. God has a better path prepared for us in Christ Jesus. Grace is given freely to those who believe in Christ alone. There will be trials, but in these trials, God will be with that person along the way. And with God in our lives, we experience great peace. Sure, there is the fear of losing a spouse in a divorce if they were to leave the church. Others in the family, and even friends may stop communicating with them for some time. This is because of new tensions that are in the air because of their departure from the church. Sure, people may start calling them up, while sending the bishop, elders, and missionaries to their homes. But all this is worth it. It may not seem this way in the beginning, but the day will come when it will. Salvation is realized when we begin to give up things for Christ's sake, although it may not be easy. This shows God that He matters more than anything else in this life. People may be upset with our decisions, but they need to know why it is necessary. To move on for the sake of Jesus and being saved, is the least we can do. This will lead you to want to be baptized in a Bible-believing church. Allowing God to become your true teacher is vital for salvation. Right now it may seem more comfortable to continue in the Mormon faith. But is it worth it to not be right with God and remain unsaved? Absolutely not. If Jesus says follow me, will people continue to follow men instead of Him? I hope not. It is better to be saved then to live a life that may seem comfortable. My friends, what is less intrusive upon our lives, are not always right for our lives in Christ Jesus.

Many people have weighed the decision of staying in the Mormon faith or leaving it behind. However, the majority have chosen to just stay in that religion for many different reasons. Resigning is out of the question to avoid a divorce, or lose their family and friends in the Mormon faith. Doing this is only digging a bigger hole for them in the afterlife. This is because once a person knows in their heart that something is wrong, they are accountable to God if they continue in it. These people were given reasons why their beliefs were wrong by way of the Bible, Christians, and the Holy Spirit. Nevertheless, they willingly turned away from the Lord. Jesus knew this and said the following. It is written, "the lord of that servant will come in a day when he looketh not for him, and at an hour when he is not aware, and will cut him in sunder, and will appoint him his portion with the unbelievers. And that servant, which knew his lord's will, and prepared not himself, neither did according to his will, shall be beaten with many stripes. But he that knew not, and did commit things worthy of stripes, shall be beaten with few stripes. For unto whomsoever much is given, of him shall be much required: and to whom men have committed much, of him they will ask the more." (Luke 12:46-48) As Jesus taught, those who die without having repented beforehand are guilty on judgment day. Come death is hell, where the lake of fire comes next after the great white throne judgment seat. Think about this outcome for a minute. Did you know that God has greater things in store for your life? He sure does, but only to those that are willing to lose everything to follow Him.

Will you give your life to follow Jesus? If so, then let me lead you in a prayer of salvation. Pray with me the following, "Father, I admit that I am a sinner and in need of a Savior. I have done wrong things and I am sorry. Forgive me, and wash me clean through the blood that You shed for us on the cross. I have believed in many things that were false, and I am sorry. Replace what is false with what is true. Help me believe in what is Biblically sound. Lead me by the Holy Spirit and to people who can help me in the faith. I am willing to learn from them. Help me find a good Bible-believing church, where I will hear sound doctrine. God, my desire is to know You, and to do what You say. I submit my life to follow You. Come into my life this day and forever. Lead me by the hand. I love You, Jesus. I give You praise! Amen." If you have prayed that prayer, then know that this is the first step of surrendering your life to Jesus. This prayer is just the beginning. Don't let your light be diminished. If you have not already, get rid of any book from Mormonism. This includes the Book of Mormon, Doctrine and Covenants, and Pearl of Great Price. Discard those books as you please, and begin reading the Bible like a child. I would recommend reading from Matthew to Revelation first. This way you will understand the kingdom and church that Jesus set apart while on earth. How his church never failed, and stands strong today. After this reading, go back to Genesis and read those books also.

The verses will make more sense after you read the New Testament. God bless you all on this new journey of following Jesus. Please know that religion does not save us but a relationship with Jesus does. Amen.

About The Author

It was the summer of 2012 that I started having doubts about the LDS Church. That summer, I was away from my family at a remote job in Nebraska. I was there for five months, but still went to Sunday services. The LDS Ward felt like a different church without the presence of my family. I felt alone, only having the bishop, and a few people saying Hi. Therefore, I sat alone and didn't feel welcome. This gave me time to reflect upon what I was taught, and also do some research to see if this church is true or not. If it was true, then why didn't people show love towards me? While feeling alone, I found websites to read and videos to watch on Mormonism. I found out different things about Joseph Smith, the first prophet of Mormonism. The unknown history of the Church. How Joseph Smith had over forty wives and even married young girls as young as fourteen. In that relationship, Joseph Smith was thirty-seven years of age. This relationship would be considered illegal. Where if there were sexual relations, it would be called "Statutory rape".

I learned about the Book of Mormon Contradictions and how it plagiarizes the Bible in many ways. How Joseph Smith had many versions of the first vision. That the Book of Abraham was found to be a false translation. How the scroll Joseph had was simply funerary texts that were deposited with mummified bodies. That Abraham was not mentioned, nor Kolob, or priesthood. After this point, doubts were swirling in my mind. For all my life, I learned that I had to be in a super quiet place to be close to the Spirit. Therefore, I thought it was normal for the church and temples to be so quiet. How I needed to obey the ordinances and laws of the Mormon Church to be saved. That I needed to pray to Heavenly Father and not Jesus for answers. Therefore, I was not close to Jesus and didn't have Him in my life. I searched for God and His truth, and thought God spoke to me at times in my life. I was hoping each Sunday that sermons would be on Jesus, but instead they were on the Temple or Joseph Smith. Joseph Smith was taught more often than even Jesus. If there was one thing that led me out of Mormonism it was the lack of Jesus and the Bible in the church. Everything else just topped it off.

It was at this time that doubts formed about the Mormon church. I went to many different websites, including YouTube, for answers. As described above, there was so much I found out that led me to rethink my faith. After all this research, I came to the realization that the church was false. I hated the fact that I went to a church that gives praise to Joseph Smith in song. So I resigned and started telling my Mormon friends and family about the problems with the LDS belief system. At that time, I felt an urgency to tell everyone I knew about the research I found. Unfortunately, the message was not received well when I presented my findings. I was told by family members to not come over anymore. Even when there were important family gatherings, I was not welcome. This was worth it, however, to be saved and leave what is comfortable behind.

In 2014, that I came across Dave Bartosiewicz's YouTube Channel. The videos were all about engaging with Mormons at the Salt Lake City Temple. He interacted with people in a way that I had never seen before. This form of evangelism appeared to be working and I paid close attention. The more I watched, the better I was able to reach the LDS people for Christ. It had a profound impact on my ability to effectively engage with Mormons and share my faith. I was fascinated by how Dave's YouTube Channel was created to guide Mormons towards Jesus. It was at this time that I started to watch Calvary Chapel on TV. Dave's videos, Calvary Chapel sermons, and other ministry videos were my go-to. It was in this timeframe that I felt God moving in my life. The next step was to find a church home for me and my family. It was at this time that I wanted to have Jesus in my life. I was willing to move on from the past and start a new life in Christ Jesus. I was finally ready to go all in for Jesus and His kingdom.

In February 2015, I decided to make the first steps of my faith in God and go to a church. That first Sunday, I got dressed and went to Calvary Chapel. The first time I set foot in the church building my heart began to swell inside. The praise music was so amazing, and I couldn't believe how wonderful I felt. I had been searching for so long for Jesus and I finally found Him. That year I was still fighting fleshly lusts and getting over bad habits, but this began to change. It was at this time that I gave my life to Jesus. Then in November of that year I felt a change in my life from God. So, I told the Lord that I wanted to be committed to serving Him. I started reading the Bible daily and praying often. My music preferences also shifted towards worship music. On December 6th, 2015, I gave my life to Jesus and got baptized. Since then, I've devoted my life to serve Him. I've been writing devotional messages and sharing them with others. This started my ministry to the Mormon people.

Many years have passed, and my ministry is in all the world. People are able to reach my content on Daily Christian Devotionals (dailycdev.com) and Christianity Vs Mormonism (christvm.com). I am continually adding new content to both websites. The content found in this book started as blog posts before making it into this book. It has taken years of research before I felt I was ready. For many years I've wanted to create this book, but never found the time. Thankfully, my research has continued, as I have much more content to share with people now. I also have an update on my family situation. We get along great. When questions come up regarding my thoughts on Mormonism, I can explain what the Bible says with respect and love. My desire in life is to follow Jesus and to draw others to Him for salvation. Jesus is my all, my everything. His love is amazing. This is the reason why I want everyone to know about the Lord and be saved. God has given me this burden to tell everyone I can about Him. Amen.

Credits

I am very grateful for the people who generously gave up their time in order to help proofread this book. The intricate process demanded attention and care, and their willingness to lend their expertise was a gift of pure benevolence. They weren't obligated to participate, but they chose to step forward. They are the unsung heroes of this literary work. The contributions they made have left an invaluable imprint on every page. Their meticulous attention to detail ensured an arduous and thorough review, leading to the rectification of grammatical errors. They went beyond just fixing punctuation and syntax, and focused on improving the overall structure and rhythm of the narrative. They refined many phrases to prove their expertise. This ensured clear and precise sentences. As we are all human, it is understandable if errors still exist.

Their discerning perspectives brought about essential modifications, allowing every word to be scrutinized under their watchful eyes. Their input produced a polished manuscript exhibiting a higher level of articulation. As a result of their relentless pursuit of perfection, the readability and articulation of this book have been significantly elevated. The nuanced improvements, the lucidity of expression and the overall flow of the narrative bear testament to their indelible efforts. It cannot be overstated that their commendable commitment is the reason behind the greater legibility of this book. This has made the contents of this book more enjoyable as chapters go on. Their vast experience and unique insights have touched and refined every part of this work. Although they wish to stay anonymous, we can all thank those who were involved with proofreading this book. May God bless them. Thank You, God, for them and for guiding me in this writing. I love You, Lord. Amen.

Other Resources

Amazon Review:

Looking forward to your Review for this book and others on Amazon.

Books:

Book Of Mormon Contradictions: Joseph's Book is Put On Trial
With The Bible
Introduction: The Book of Mormon is placed in the courtroom of
scrutiny, with the Bible as the source of truth. Each individual verse

in the Book of Mormon is effectively put on trial. The Bible serves as the frame of reference for the trial at hand. This is very important, as we do not want to be led astray through a fictional book that is said to be scripture. In saying this, I have compared the verses in the Book of Mormon with the Bible and found that many verses disagree with the Biblical text. These verses will be looked over in great detail, in order to properly understand the issues we are dealing with. Instead of the two books complimenting each other, we see them contradicting one another in many ways. An in-depth analysis of the Book of Mormon shows a substantial amount of problems that cannot be denied. As you traverse through the chapters of this book, the problems in the Book of Mormon will be readily seen. These disparities come to life, seeing what the Bible actually teaches compared to the Book of Mormon. Most teachings are not the same. If they are, then they contradict the teachings in Mormonism.

Free to read and listen to:

https://christvm.com/learn/christian-books/table-of-contents-bomc/

Purchase:
https://www.amazon.com/dp/B0CQKMHQ7Q

Book Of Mormon Plagiarism: Parts Of The KJV Bible Were Plagiarized

Introduction: Why are so many verses in the Book of Mormon taken from the King James Bible? For example, verses from the Book of Isaiah are found all throughout this book. One compelling argument for this viewpoint is that Lehi and his family left Jerusalem 100 years after Isaiah died. This is how they acquired his writings. It would make sense if the writings were on scrolls, but instead they are on plates of brass. The Isaiah Scrolls were discovered among the Dead Sea scrolls. According to the findings, people were writing on scrolls and not brass plates. So to say that the Book of Isaiah was written down on plates makes you wonder if Mormons ever heard of the Dead Sea scrolls. We have evidence that this book, and other old writings, were recorded on ancient scrolls. They were also stored in various types of jars for sake keeping. Therefore, it doesn't make sense to have the Book of Isaiah written on brass plates. And what about the golden plates for the Book of Mormon? If Bible authors wrote on plates, then where is the evidence? Have golden plates ever been found with writings from people of old? The answer is No.

Free to read and listen to:

https://christvm.com/learn/christian-books/table-of-contents-bom p/

Purchase:
https://www.amazon.com/dp/B0CRBLBKJS

Joseph Smith Changed The Bible: Revelation

Introduction: A Bible translation from an ancient manuscript is acceptable if the person is led by God. This means that he or she understands both languages also. Those who rewrite an already translated Bible are not led by God. Any paraphrased version of a translated Biblical text should be thrown out and not read. One such version of the Bible is the Joseph Smith Translation. This is where Joseph Smith used the King James Bible to write his own translation. It is written, "Joseph Smith, the first prophet of The Church of Jesus Christ of Latter-day Saints, made a "new translation" of the Bible, using the text of the King James Version (KJV). This work differs from the KJV in at least 3,410 verses and consists of additions, deletions, rearrangements, and other alterations that cause it to vary not only from the KJV but from other biblical texts." (Joseph Smith Translation of the Bible, JST) This quote comes from the byu.edu website.

Free to read and listen to:

https://christvm.com/learn/christian-books/table-of-contents-jscb/

Purchase:

https://www.amazon.com/dp/B0CWD736ZN

Facebook:

Paul Gee

Sharing the good news of Jesus. My Facebook page is dedicated to telling people about Jesus and leading those who are lost to Him. I have been using this social media platform since 2015 for the glory of God.

https://www.facebook.com/paul.gee.332

Christianity Vs Mormonism Group

In this group, you will find people of all walks of life. Those who are LDS, Christian, seekers of truth, atheists, agnostics, and more. The reason to have this group is to bring what is true to the attention of others through the Bible. If we were taught wrong to concede and learn from others. The Bible is our source of truth, so put aside what is false and trust in what is true. This is also a great place to witness to those who are lost, like the Mormon people.

https://www.facebook.com/groups/christvm

Websites:

Daily Christian Devotionals

Growing closer to Jesus daily! I started this ministry of writing daily devotionals in 2015. Over the course of that time and until now, I have written almost three thousand full-length devotionals. These messages cover every book from the Bible, and almost every topic you can think of. So many messages are on praise, marriage, Jesus being God, and so much more. There are dozens of charts, music, videos, and evangelism resources also. I've made everything free and without ads. All for the glory of God.

dailycdev.com

Christianity Vs Mormonism

Only Jesus saves, not religion! I started this ministry in 2016 while witnessing to Mormons via social media and on the streets. It was in 2017 that my friend Patrick invited me to go on a mission trip to Utah, which I said yes to. Since that time, we have been going to the LDS General Conference twice a year. I have passed out thousands of handouts with regard to this site. They contain the differences in Christianity compared to Mormonism, as well as many charts. Everything is free on this site, including books. All the glory to God. christvm.com

YouTube Channel:

Truth In Jesus

Every other Saturday there is a new topic that I discuss with a variety of Christians and Mormons. These shows are set up in a debate format where people have time to talk if needed. All I ask is that people be respectful in how they treat each other while discussing their point. This channel is meant to lead people to the real Jesus of the Bible and to showcase this through the Bible. Opinions don't matter, but what God's Word says. That is why I continually use Bible passages in the videos to prove my points. God bless you all. Amen.

https://www.youtube.com/channel/UCA8p5VHFLuZic0e0ohf9Fs g

Made in the USA
Columbia, SC
28 August 2024